Excerpts from
THE RISE OF ANTICHRIST

You may think it is science fiction but one day it is conceivable that parents will go to a *"genetic supermarket"* for gene seeds mixed to their specification. Russia has jumped into this race with all fervency. Chapter 1

* * *

World leaders whose ambition is for greater power know that if they can control the mind they can control the population. What a ripe opportunity for Antichrist to make man a chemically controlled machine! Chapter 3

* * *

Hitler ran *"fertilization farms"* in an effort to create a superior race. Now Russia and China are following a similar pattern to control the world. Chapter 4

* * *

Antichrist would select certain key people. After giving them positions of authority he would demand that, in order to retain that power, they submit to having two electrodes planted in their brains. One electrode would go to the pleasure center . . . the other to the pain center. Chapter 5

* * *

Scientists have discovered that memories can be <u>transferred</u>! And not only that, now memories can be <u>erased</u>! Our drinking water could be the carrier. Chapter 6

* * *

Sperm banks are becoming increasingly popular. Shipments are made worldwide. It is entirely possible that a woman will be able to buy a tiny frozen embryo and have it implanted in her uterus. Studies are now being considered of gestating human babies in cows! Chapter 8

* * *

One biologist advocates granting two marketable *"baby licenses"* to each family only after they pass qualifying tests approved by the Government. Chapter 9

* * *

Rand Corporation scientists estimate that by the year 2005, human cloning will be widespread. One could produce identical aggressive, rugged soldiers as predictably as stamping out nuts and bolts. Chapter 10

* * *

All this and much more you will find in the 23 ~~chapters~~ ~~of this~~ ~~ex~~citing and revealing book that provides y~~ou~~ ~~~~ how close we are to the Rapture and t~~~~ ~~~~ <u>rela-tion come alive!</u>

THE RISE
OF
ANTICHRIST

by Salem Kirban

Second Printing .... October, 1979
Third Printing .... April, 1980

Library of Congress Catalog Card No. 78-58625
ISBN 0-912582-29-4

DEDICATION

To **Darrell Kirban**
Jessica Frick
Joshua Frick

our grandchildren,
who face a world of uncertainty,
but whose safety rests
in an abiding faith in Jesus Christ.

To **Mani Veerasamy**
Eddie Shi
Taunga Tumu
Marshall Masai
Phil Whelton
Iotia Nooroa

students at Prairie Bible Institute,
who face a world filled with increasing trials and tensions. They
represent tomorrow's vanguard of disciplined soldiers for Christ
. . . ready to serve Him . . . in any corner of the globe!

ACKNOWLEDGMENTS

To **Doreen Frick,** who carefully proofread the text.

To **Walter W. Slotilock,** Chapel Hill Litho, for skillfully making the illustration negatives.

To **Batsch Company, Inc.,** for excellent craftsmanship in setting the type quickly.

To **Koechel Designs,** who designed the front cover and chapter art.

CONTENTS

WHY I WROTE THIS BOOK

In the last few years the world has suffered agonizing pains of constant turmoil ... from terrorist activities in Europe and the United States to wars in the Middle East and Africa.

The United States has fallen into Russia's subtle trap in the game of détente. And Russia's military power has increased to a point where she could well control outer space!

Meanwhile although the United States economy is bursting at the seams, the purchasing power of the dollar is rapidly diminishing! It is entirely possible that the United States will be forced to join the Common Market nations in an alliance to protect them from the threat of world Communism. Such an alliance, in my opinion, will probably occur before the year 2000.

One of the tragedies of today is that we do not learn from history. Many can still remember the tyranny of Adolf Hitler and his ability to deceive millions of Jews . . . to the point of having them walk like sheep to their slaughter. They met their death quietly in gas chambers while other nations looked on either in disbelief or unconcern.

We are at that point again in history. And not even born again Christians appear to be aware of how critical is the hour we now live. No, we are not seeing gas chambers and ovens being used. But we are witnessing something even more deadly . . . mind manipulation.

Right now the MIND MANIPULATORS are at work devising methods to control human life, to control human behaviour, and to make the general population walking, obedient robots. We are on the brink of the Rapture and the Tribulation Period.

The tragedy is that many Church leaders are more concerned about building mansions here on earth then reaching the lost with the Gospel of Jesus Christ.

The world is seeking peace. It is looking for a Superman. But peace will never be achieved by man. The curtain of tomorrow may soon be lifted, however, to reveal a man whose peace will unleash an avalanche of terror . . . such as the world has never seen. Right now, this very moment, we are witnesses to events that will bring **THE RISE OF ANTICHRIST!** That's why I wrote this book!

Salem Kirban

Huntingdon Valley, Pennsylvania
U.S.A., June, 1978

1

THE DAY THEY RESHAPE MAN

"Good afternoon ladies and gentlemen. This is your pilot speaking. We are flying at an altitude of 35,000 feet and a speed of 700 miles an hour. I have two pieces of news to report, one good and one bad. The bad news is that we are lost. The good news is that we are making excellent time."

On The
Threshold
of
Catastrophe

This could well reflect the dilemma of today's scientists. They are on the threshold of human catastrophe . . . a catastrophe that is creating the climate for Antichrist! Actually, we are already living in the age of Antichrist. Now, don't get me wrong. I have no inside information that Antichrist is already here. (Although, privately, I believe he is living today.)

And most certainly, the **forces** of Antichrist are here!

We are already living within the realm of the possibility of programming human behavior, manipulating genes and the uniform packaging of people as neatly as one would package the uniform potato chip, *Pringles!*

Behavioral psychologists are finding new ways to reshape people and control their behavior. One geneticist asked the U.S. Congress to appropriate $10 million to set up a national genetic task force.

Genetic engineering is a new term with frightening implications. Just what is a "gene?"

A *gene* is the part of a cell that determines the characteristics living things inherit from their parents. Genes determine such features as the shape of a leaf or the sex, height, and hair color of a child.

Genes are located in the innermost part of a cell called the nucleus, and make up orderly units of threadlike chromosomes. There are thousands of genes in every cell!

DNA
And
RNA
Engineering

Genes produce their effect by influencing chemical and physical processes during growth. Genes are primarily made up of deoxyribonucleic acid **(DNA)**. DNA is one of the nucleic acids in the nucleus of every cell.

Genes of some viruses are made up of ribonucleic acid **(RNA)**.

Now, when you read about **DNA** and **RNA**

engineering by geneticists you will have some idea of the tragic consequences that will occur as man attempts to control and alter genes.

Think for a moment! If someone could control the formation of genes or manipulate them to his advantage, one could conceivably control a large segment of the human race! On the other hand, because of the complexity of their structure . . . such experimentation could lead to monstrosities and robots.

Prelude To Tribulation

Now does the judgment of the Fifth Trumpet during the Tribulation Period seem more plausible to you? During this judgment strange beings described as *"locusts"* plague the world. They look like horses armed for battle yet they have faces that look like men and long hair like women. Read Revelation 9:3-12.

Up until a few years ago scientists were not aware that genes could be manipulated. In the mid-1940's experiments at the Rockefeller Institute revealed the acid now known as DNA. It was later discovered that this could be considered the <u>master molecule of life</u>!

Two young biologists at Cambridge University then discovered that the DNA molecule resembled a spiraling staircase. The banisters of this staircase are made of sugars and phosphates . . . the stair treads of four organic compounds: <u>a</u>denine,

Will it be possible for scientists to manipulate genes to produce a strange being that resembles the "locusts" of Revelation 9:3-12?

guanine, thymine and cytosine. They called these four compounds **AGTC**. This constitutes the genetic code.

Biologist Jean Rostand states:

> The properties of an individual's heredity depend on the way in which those four bases are arranged and ordered in their molecules; all the genetic diversity of the species stems from them, just as all our literature is written with twenty-six letters and all our music with seven notes.

Breaking The Gene Code

Now this may seem a little complicated to you but it is important that you understand what a gene is. For if scientists can break the code that is used in forming a person . . . his physical appearance, his temperament, his intelligence . . . scientists can then manipulate genes to produce a man or woman to fit their whims. **This then becomes the day they can reshape man into the image they want him.** And such a possibility fits into the pattern that is conducive to the emergence of an Antichrist!

Whether you realize it or not gene scientists are hot on the trail for an answer to controlling genes. They can already manipulate them and they have developed techniques known as gene-splicing. Gene-splicing enables them to transplant genetic information from one unrelated creature to another.

Design Your Own Baby

You may think it is science fiction but one day it is conceivable that parents will go to a "genetic supermarket" for gene seeds mixed to their specification.

From infants to adulthood, Chinese men and women are manipulated into a pattern of conforming, in action, in dress and in allegiance to Chairman Mao's "correct thinking" as outlined in the Red Book.

I would personally recommend that every concerned individual read The People Shapers by Vance Packard. It will open your eyes!

Genetic Counselors Increasing

There are already over 1000 genetic counselors in the United States. In 1951 there were only about 10.

Genetic scientists fully aware of the monster they could be creating urged their fellow scientists to exercise self-restraint. *Science News* reported:

> Both by accident and by purposeful manipulation, genes for drug resistance or cancer or lethal toxin formation could be inserted into common organisms. Biological warfare agents and massive epidemics could be created too effectively.

But now the race is on. And Russia has jumped in with an all-out fervency, as have other nations, to win the race of the manipulation of man. Where will it lead? It will lead to the age of Antichrist!

For the scientist . . . the good news is that they are making excellent time.

The bad news is that they are lost!

2

THE PLAN TO CONTROL THE HUMAN MIND

Listen to some of the statements of scientists who are *"human engineers"* and you would think you were in fantasyland. But the sad fact is that they mean what they say and they are determined to control all aspects of human life not only after it is born but <u>before</u> it is born . . . and even more frightening . . . <u>before</u> ovulation occurs!

One behavioral psychologist from Harvard University, remarked:

We need to make vast changes in human behavior.

Another has urged the United States government to make *"conquering the mind"* a national goal.

In his research on the subject, Vance Packard remarked:

Some of the projects to reshape or control Man . . . are disturbing. Some may make your skin crawl . . . such plans as keeping people under surveillance by locking transmitters to their bodies, creating subhumans for menial work . . . transplanting heads . . . pacifying troublesome people, including children, by cutting into the brain.[1]

The Day
They
Control
Life

---

[1] Vance Packard, <u>The People Shapers</u> (Boston: Little, Brown and Company) 1977, p. 253.

H. L. Newbold, in his book *The Psychiatric Programming of People,* makes the revealing statement:

> *Man is, for psychological purposes, a computer.*

Making Man A Computer

Many psychiatrists, psychologists and scientists think of man as a machine . . . a machine that can be manipulated if one knows the proper code for the manipulation process.

Manipulation in its crudest forms is not new. Adolf Hitler was a master of manipulation in his hypnotizing of millions of Germans. But we can recognize this quite easily. However, in our more sophisticated 1980 society, we will be seeing a more subtle and much more dangerous approach to the manipulation of man. It will culminate with Antichrist.

Television is a master media of mind manipulation. Advertisers know that children control the majority of purchasing power for such things as breakfast cereals, cookies, candy and toys. Actually, children consume at least $75 billion worth of products in the United States. And by subliminal seduction they are manipulated to fulfill the desires of the advertisers.

Subliminal means *"below the threshold of consciousness."* This involves the use of stimuli that become effective subconsciously by repetition. Advertisers know

Although viewers did not see the message flashed on the screen, they obeyed the compelling impulse to purchase both popcorn and cola.

that the mind is quicker than the eye! The mind can go to Mars and back in an instant. The eye (or light) takes minutes.

Initial experiments with subliminal seduction involved the use of a tachistoscope. This is a film projector with a high-speed shutter which flashes messages every five seconds but at 1/3000th of a second! This was first used in motion picture theaters or upon film being transmitted through television.

Now, remember this, the high-speed messages were **invisible** to the conscious mind. However, they planted messages in the viewer's unconscious mind and got results.

Wilson Bryan Key reports:

> *During one six-week test of a machine in a theater, involving 45,699 patrons, messages were flashed on alternate days:*
>
> <u>Hungry? Eat Popcorn</u>
>
> *and*
>
> <u>Drink Coca-Cola</u>
>
> *During the six weeks, popcorn sales increased 57.7 percent and Coca Cola sales 18.1 percent.*[1]

Food companies are masters in a subtle type of mind manipulation. Over 500 new products are introduced every month! The average supermarket stocks more than 7000 products! Yet a few companies control the majority of the products. Beatrice Foods, as an example, derives more than

---

[1]Wilson Bryan Key, <u>Subliminal Seduction</u> (New Jersey: Prentice-Hall, Inc.) 1973, p. 23

$5.2 billion a year from more than 8000 products. They include Dannon Yogurt, Swiss Miss Cocoa, the LaChoy line of oriental foods and numerous cakes and candies.

Advertisers spend over $30 billion a year to mold and influence the consumption habits of Americans.

Testing The Blink Rate

With such an investment, naturally food companies want their products to sell. Package designs become vitally important. And techniques are used in such designs and in marketing that subtly (yet legally) persuade or manipulate an individual's actions. Some companies have used hidden cameras behind their products to check the "*blink rate*" of the shopper as he or she passed by. If the eyes blinked slowly, the package design was considered a success because it hypnotized the consumer.

With over 2500 additives in our food many people do not realize that this becomes a form of mind control.

Tranquilized Youngsters

Ben F. Feingold, an allergist, studied hyperkinetic children at the Kaiser-Permanente Medical Center in central California. He, as well as many nutritionists before him, began to realize that much of the abnormal child behavior was due to artificial food colors and additives. While this was tragic enough, it was the rebound that caused real tragedy and evidenced how human behavior is controlled.

Teachers in Omaha, Nebraska, seeking a

solution to misbehavior in class, sought advice. Some advice given by representatives of drug companies related how pills could help children concentrate and perform better in class.

Pills in Lunch Buckets

In Omaha several thousand children were carrying pills in their lunch buckets. The pills were stimulants . . . amphetamines or Ritalin. Some of the side effects of Ritalin in children are:

> loss of appetite
> abdominal pain
> weight loss
> insomnia

Science Digest estimated that as many as 2 million children were taking these mind-changers.

It was fortunate that Dr. Feingold revealed his findings.

Certainly subliminal seduction and food additives are evils of this 20th century society and contribute to mind control. But they are not as tragic nor convey the potentiality of horror as some other aspects of mind manipulation.

The plan to control the human mind is a well organized plan. And all major powers are furiously working on systems that will benefit their personal goals.

Mass Media Persuasion

One must not overlook the mass media such as television and the press. We are living in the age of conglomerates. We now have newspaper chains under single ownership. Television networks own other properties of communication. It may surprise you to know that Word Records is owned by the American Broadcasting Company, as an example.

The Sin of Omission

The media can control your thoughts, your emotions and manipulate you to mold your opinions.

The minute Watergate is mentioned . . . you already have a preconceived opinion . . . molded initially by a prominent Washington newspaper. It was effective in dethroning a President. Such television programs as *60 Minutes* and other news programs quickly mold public opinion. They do not necessarily tell an untruth in reporting the news. But by the **omission** of some facts, it is easy to *"stack"* a news program into any direction the interviewer desires. Such reporting becomes misleading reporting and hearkens back to the days of yellow journalism. Today, however, it is much more subtle . . . much more deceiving and much more effective!

You say your mind is not being controlled? As a born-again Christian, with a foundation in the Word of God . . . you are not being deceived, you claim?

You may be surprised! I am amazed how many Christians are deceived by what they see on television, and what they read. I am amazed at how many believers are manipulated by the world.

You
Believe
A
Lie!

I have often said in my Bible prophecy messages:

I can go through your shopping cart, housewife, and I can show you how that over 90% of the products you buy, you buy because you have believed a lie!

If it is so easy for you to believe the little lies of today . . . how much easier it will be for Antichrist to tell the BIG LIE in the Tribulation Period . . . because

God shall send them strong delusion that they should believe a lie.
                    (2 Thessalonians 2:11 KJV)

The plan to control the human mind is a last ditch desperate plan concocted by the forces of evil and directed in its final scene by Antichrist.

3

MAKING MAN A CHEMICALLY CONTROLLED MACHINE

The Bible reveals that during the Tribulation Period that Antichrist:

> . . . causes all,
> the small and the great,
> and the rich and the poor,
> and the free man and the slaves,
> to be given a mark
> on their right hand,
> or on their forehead,
>
> and he provides that no one
> should be able to buy or to sell,
> except the one who has the mark,
> either the name of the beast (Antichrist)
> or the number of his name.
>
> (Revelation 13:16-17 NASV)

We are further told that the number of his name is **666.**

Subtle Force

Now I am sure that not everyone living during this time will want to take on this Mark. But the coercive system at the time will compel them to do so. When they see their children crying and then getting sick because of a lack of food; when they rush their children to the hospital and are turned away . . . such pressure will "encourage" them to give in and accept the Mark. It will be impossible to survive without this "license to live."

And by accepting the Mark they will take the first step in being reprogrammed into the mold that Antichrist desires.

People the world over, and particularly Americans, are already being conditioned for this new world system that will be under Antichrist. They may appear to be to you subtle little things that have no significance. But block upon block, they are stepping stones that are eventually paving the way for the Antichrist Mark on your right hand or forehead.

Destroying
Identity

Think how many things in your life have been reduced to numbers. Hitler knew that the first objective in brainwashing was to destroy a person's identity. The Nazis tattooed numbers on the arms of millions of Jews. They were forbidden to use their name. They had to use their number. This was the first step to whip them into submission and conformity.

This number became the universal identifier. Holland was proud of its super identification system it had installed prior to World War 2. Every citizen had a number. But France, easy going, kept very haphazard records of individuals . . . loose and slipshod.

What happened? When the Nazis invaded Holland they captured the files that con-

The day will come when a hospital will refuse admittance to a mother with a sick child because neither bears the Mark of Antichrist.

tained the numbering codes and tracked down all the Jews in Holland. It was the numbers that led them to arrest the father of Anne Frank. Now, in France, it was a different matter. That is why many Jewish people fled to France for safety.

Trend Towards The Mark

Towns are now known by zip code. Phone exchanges are now numbers, not names. Products in supermarkets are now identified by a number and line marking system. The Government knows you by a number. One major Christian college I know assigns a number to each student. When he walks into the auditorium each day, he calls out his number to the monitor. Your most universal number is now your Social Security Number. Quite conceivably it could become the Mark. Technology is already here whereby the Social Security Number could be painlessly imprinted on your forehead or right hand in invisible ink revealed only by a special light.

The Government Computer

The Internal Revenue Service planned for the development of a nationwide $850 million computer for monitoring taxpayers. This massive data processing system with 8300 terminals would make it possible for some 48,300 IRS employees to have almost instantaneous access to the records of individuals and corporations.

In February, 1978, the Carter administration halted the plans for this computer giant because of opposition from Con-

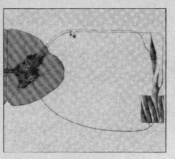

Valium and other mood changing drugs are widely misused. They affect the brain. Over 40% of women in America have used such drugs and over 25% of all men. And the tragedy is that the use of tranquilizers is growing. Such a trend will make any nation more susceptible to the pressures exerted by Antichrist during the Tribulation Period. It will be easy to make them subservient robots.

gress. However, one day, such a plan will become a reality.

World leaders whose ambition is for greater power know that if they can control the mind they can control the population. Russia has been moderately successful in this. But, unable to become completely successful, they have had to resort to crude force. They did this in Hungary. They did it in Berlin when they built the Berlin Wall.

Drugs Destroy Initiative

How can you control the mind? Their first step is to recognize that man can become a machine . . . a controlled machine through a chemical process. Valium is a typical example of a mood-changing drug. In 1977, doctors in the United States wrote approximately 60 million prescriptions for Valium, resulting in retail sales of over half a billion dollars. Despite Valium's vast popularity, little is understood about how it works and even less about the condition it is taken to combat.

Valium is made up of aniline which comes from nitrobenzene. Nitrobenzene is prepared by treating benzene with a mixture of nitric and sulfuric acids. The second component is benzoic acid which comes from toluene, a petroleum product. The third component is glycine, an amino acid. The fourth component is the addition of the methyl group, achieved by treating the compound with caustic soda and dimethylsulfate. The dimethylsulfate is obtained by treating chlorosulfonic acid with methyl alcohol, commonly known as wood alcohol. That is Valium! And in any given year, 20% of all American women and 14% of men will use the drug.

Continued use of tranquilizers can cause slow, rhythmic, involuntary movement of the tongue and facial muscles and uncontrolled movement of the arms, legs and trunk.

Depression Before Submission

Whatever your personal opinion is about Valium, you can see that this and other mood changing drugs can work to the benefit of Antichrist. If he can get most of the population to forget about their troubles and struggle for living, by swallowing a pill, his battle is almost already won for complete dominance of the nations.

The brain has about 10 billion working cells, which are called neurons. They weigh only six ounces! Anyone who can exercise some control over these *"action"* cells can control the human being! Mood changing drugs such as Valium depress these cells and give one *"the devil-may-care attitude."* They make one much more vulnerable to conformity.

Tranquilized Through Your Water

This chemical control can also be added through our drinking water, without our knowledge. A population could be kept docile, and subjugated to the powers in control, by dosing the drinking water with a tranquilizing chemical.

Or they may wish to add some aggression-inciting chemical to the drinking water . . .

or for that matter, even to the air we breathe!

Most people don't even know what is already in the water they drink! They would be surprised if they had it analyzed. Many communities have added fluorides to the water, as an example. This decision made by a few, is imposed on an entire community.

How easy, when a world leader wants to launch a massive propaganda campaign, for buckets of a specified chemical to be dumped in strategic water basins designed to produce the desired conforming effects! Fantasy? Absolutely not. Entirely possible today!

Why Tranquilizers

How many leaders can you count in your own church who are already taking tranquilizers and look like walking pill boxes? And yet we are the people who claim the Blessed Hope! We are the ones who should rest in God and cast all our burdens on Him. But, in reality, how many actually do that? Be honest. What about yourself? Do you find yourself dependent on drugs to give you a state of euphoria? Or do you look to the Saviour to give you peace of mind and freedom from fear? You may be surprised to find out how many Pastors are taking mood-changing drugs!

Now, what I am saying is this. If Christians are hooked on mood-changing drugs, in spite of the hope that is within us through

Jesus Christ, how much more widespread is the use of mood-changing drugs by those whose only hope is living for today!

What a tragic situation!

And what a ripe opportunity for Antichrist to make man a chemically controlled machine, a slave to his whim and call, to do his bidding.

If the nation is already tranquilized . . . can the day of infamy be far behind?

4

THE BRAIN THAT'S NOT YOUR OWN

Steps
To
Control
Your
Brain

Right now, you are a free agent. You are reading this book because you want to. You didn't think anything about that privilege. In fact, I doubt that you consider it a privilege that you can make your own decisions.

Your brain sent you signals and you sat down and decided to read this book. You can decide to continue reading this chapter. Or you can set the book down and go to the kitchen and get a sandwich. You control your actions.

Your moods are your own. Perhaps right now you are happy. Or you may be frustrated. Or you may be angry. Whatever your mood, you are, in a sense, in control of your moods.

Now think for a moment.

**Drugs
Alter
Brain
Function**

Do you realize that right now it is technically possible for someone else to control your brain!

Such scientific advances have been made in brain control that if they were exercised on your brain . . .

> You would not be able to sit down and read this book, at your pleasure.
>
> You would not be able to get up and go to the kitchen to get a sandwich, when you wished.
>
> If you were happy with your wife and family, a simple action by an outside force could <u>suddenly</u> change your brain patterns and turn you into an angry, aggressive husband with a power to kill, yes, even your loved ones!

In other words, your brain although your own, would be controlled by someone else! This is not futuristic thinking. This technology is already a very workable reality. And right now behavior specialists the world over are experimenting with brain control devices.

The brain can be made to function in many different ways. Each way produces a different private world.

**The
Master
Organ**

Drugs alter experience by their effect on brain function. Tranquilizers, as an example, dull that part of the brain where emotions are created. This is the <u>limbic</u> system of the brain.

The brain is the master organ of your body. The brain is not a single organ but has many parts with special functions, though they are all connected.

The brain has three main divisions:

1. The forebrain
2. The midbrain
3. The hindbrain

The forebrain contains the <u>cerebrum</u>. The cerebrum is the largest and most important part of the human brain. It makes up about 85% of the brain weight.

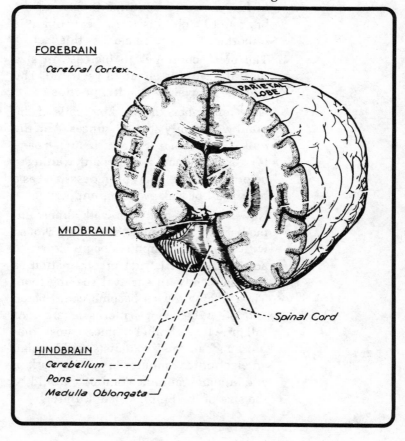

<u>FOREBRAIN</u>
Cerebral Cortex

PARIETAL LOBE

<u>MIDBRAIN</u>

Spinal Cord

<u>HINDBRAIN</u>
Cerebellum
Pons
Medulla Oblongata

The cerebrum consists of two halves, resembling a half a shelled walnut. Each hemisphere of the cerebrum is divided into five lobes. One of these lobes is the limbic. The limbic is the center of emotion and memory.

Controlling The Center of Emotion

And it is this area where "*behavior engineers*" devote much of their energies.

The brain weighs less than a pound at birth, or about a tenth of the body weight. In fact new cells continue to form in the brain until a child is 1 or 2 years old. It is important that you remember this fact.

The brain continues to increase in size until the child is about 15 years old. The adult brain weighs about 3 pounds.

Now remember, the working cells of the brain weigh only about 6 ounces. And the bulk of the brain of a newborn human baby is like a brand new switchboard, waiting to be programmed. It has been described as a blank ball of wax awaiting impressions.

Now a horse at birth can walk almost immediately . . . as can most animals. Not so with man. His computers begin slowly to acquire skills. His first preoccupation as an infant, is with survival seeking food. Then later his eyes become coordinated and other behavior patterns emerge. At full growth his brain becomes a most complex mechanism. If scientists could design an electronic computer to do the work of one human brain, the computer would be the size of the Empire State Building.

**The
Critical
Time**

Those engaged in the study of genetics and control of human behavior know that the critical period for imprinting behavior patterns run from about six weeks to six months after birth.

Now stop here a minute and consider the importance of the last statement. Can you see why Hitler ran *"fertilization farms"* where women conceived and had children in an effort to create a superior race. What happened after they gave birth. The mothers were sent back to work and the babies were cared for by the state, under controlled conditions, to program them for life.

What other countries follow a similar pattern today? Russia and China. Both of these countries have 80% or more of their women working. When they bear children, those children are taken care of in day nurseries by the State. Emotional and physical contact is severely limited. And the mind imprinting procedures begin at this early age.

**Plastic
Children**

When a child becomes school age, if he is in China, he carries the Red Book of Chairman Mao, like your children would carry a New Testament or Bible. Because the imprinting begins right after birth, a reversal becomes next to impossible. Thus the building of a race whose emotions and memories and moods are all geared to the State and to loyal, unwavering obedience.

Once a mother gives birth to a child at a "fertilization farm" she will be forced to leave the baby in a nursery controlled by Antichrist.

Japan, prior to World War 2 followed this principle of child rearing. And you may recall how Kamikaze pilots willingly volunteered for suicide attacks on American ships . . . using themselves and their plane as the human bomb, for the Emperor!

Right now, you believe your brain is your own. And to a vast extent, it most certainly is.

The Frightening Future

But have you ever stopped to think already how highly impressionable it is to subtle motivations from the press, from the government, from the drugs you take, and from the foods you eat that contain additives that can change your moods?

Now these are child's play in controlling brain actions compared to what lies in store for those living 20 to 30 years from now.

Right now, experiments are being conducted to dig into the vast reservoir of the brain, to map it for ultimate control . . . a control that can make you a walking robot manipulated by an Antichrist.

By the way,
Who's that behind you?

5

CONTROLLING THE BRAIN THROUGH SURGERY

Did you look around after you read:

Who's that behind you?

If you did, you can see how easy the power of suggestion even can manipulate the brain!

Brain surgery is a highly selective skill. Much of it has saved lives. Some has been unnecessary. Experimental brain surgery on animals in laboratories worldwide has some frightening consequences if placed in the hands of evil men.

James Olds, while at McGill University, pioneered in brain probing in his experiments with rats. This psychologist accidentally discovered that the brain could be activated by an electrical stimulant.

Choose
Your
Mood

This discovery inspired a researcher at Tulane University to develop a self-stimulator for man. Conceivably this portable device would be strapped to the waist. Electrodes would be implanted in the brain. By pushing some buttons an individual could activate these electrodes to modify his mood at will. He would push a *"happy"* button, an *"aggressive"* button or any of the *"pleasure"* buttons to control his emotions. In experiments with this unit patients were run through the gamut of moods from sexually active to feeling sick all over.

In fact, José M. R. Delgado, a behavioral scientist, who spent many years at Yale and now directs research at a new institute in Madrid, states:

> *Predictable behavioral and mental responses may be induced by direct manipulation of the brain.*

Losing
The
Mother
Instinct

He was able to demonstrate this by a strategically placed ten-second electrical stimulation to a mother monkey named Rose. Usually the mother of a baby rhesus monkey devotes months in affection for her baby. But when Delgado electrically stimulated the brain of the mother monkey she not only lost interest in her baby but ignored the tender calls of the baby and, in fact, rejected attempts by the baby to approach her!

What a heartbreak this would be to you, if you were a young mother, and also to your child. And this is the direction we are going. A plan to break family bonds . . . first through day nurseries and then by implanted electrodes that will control your love instincts and make you repel those you love!

A loving mother cuddles her baby exercising all the motherly instincts.

With the press of a control button, the mother can be made to reject her child, refuse to love or feed it!

This is one of the methods in which brain surgery can manipulate an entire nation or nations under one dictator.

Electrodes In The Brain

Antichrist would select certain key people to be on his staff. Then after giving them positions of authority demand that in order to retain their power they would have to submit to having two electrodes planted in their brains. One electrode would go to the pleasure center. And this would certainly excite the worldly and carnally minded. The other electrode, however, would go to the pain center.

With a promise of unending vistas of pleasure never before experienced, you can imagine how many would quickly accept these electrodes even though the consequences of pain were also possible.

Researcher Vance Packard reports that an electronic engineer at a national electronics conference revealed:

> A baby could have a socket holding electrodes planted on or in his brain within a few months of birth and "the once-human being thus controlled would be the cheapest of machines to create and operate."[1]

The Ice Pick Operation

Surgery to change the mind and man's actions is not new. It has been practiced in the United States for years. It is called a lobotomy. In a lobotomy fibers between the frontol lobes and deeper portions of the brain are severed.

---

[1]Vance Packard, The People Shapers (Boston: Little, Brown and Company) 1977, p. 60

Above advertisement appeared in publications in May, 1978 announcing a new book, In His Image. Author claims that a cloned baby has already been produced. Whether this is true or not, scientists are getting closer to their goal of being able to manipulate genes to reproduce identical human beings in the exact image of the donor.

Lobotomy operations increased rapidly after World War 2. Thousands were performed on returning soldiers to *"correct"* disturbed veterans.

The operation became very simplified. Soon some surgeons were simply running an ice pick-type device up past the eyeball and wiggling it around for a while. Doctors could perform ten or twelve such lobotomies in a few hours. One doctor has done several thousand. This has become a highly controversial subject even among doctors. Some of these patients became *"vegetables."* And while it corrected some behavior patterns, the side effects were worse than the original problem.

Similar brain surgery has been done on children who were termed hyperactive, emotionally unstable or aggressive.

Remember a lobotomy does not require extensive surgery such as cutting open the brain. It can be done quickly and leaves no visible scars simply by introducing an ice pick-type device up past the eyeball into the brain. What a tool in the hands of Antichrist.

Controlling Your Method Of Giving Birth

But besides dulling initiative and individualism, Antichrist will want to develop some super brains he can control. And, yes, some research has been going on in this direction as well.

Geneticists have come to the conclusion that the shape of the human female pelvis puts a limit on the size of the infant skull. Because the skull is limited in size, so is the human brain.

Now, if the baby did not have to come down through the cervix, which dilates to about 4 inches, the brain quite possibly could be larger.

**A Decree
For
Caesarean
Delivery**

Think ahead for a moment. Suppose Antichrist issued a decree that from now on all births would be by Caesarean delivery. Quite possibly, through heredity in future generations the brain might grow larger. Now suppose Antichrist speeds up this process by injecting growth hormones while the mother is pregnant . . . such an end product could be accelerated!

A French biologist who is a Nobel prize winner, suggested that drugs could be developed that either speed up or slow down cell divisions in the prenatal brain. In this way larger brains via Caesarean delivery could be assured.

One brain physiologist stated:

> I certainly could educate a child by putting an electrode in the lateral hypothalamus and then selecting the situations at which I stimulate it. In this way I can grossly change his behavior.

I believe that initial tampering with the brain will be to seduce the population into believing they will be sharing in a better world . . . a world of complete pleasure devoid of depression. But like the web of the spider, once entrapped, that individual will lose all control of his actions. He will be controlled by someone else. That someone else could be Antichrist!

6

THE DAY THEY TRANSPLANT MEMORIES

Some new discoveries have been made by psychologists regarding memory. These revelations have left many scientists alarmed because of the ulterior possibilities of controlling man.

Opening Pandora's Box

When one begins to alter God's creation, man, through mood and mind control and manipulation of genes, one opens a literal Pandora's box.

You may remember this was a myth about a woman who, in curiosity, opened a box, letting out all human ills into the world.

We believe that our memories are personal. They are ours. They cannot be transferred. They are private.

Not so!

Scientists have discovered that memories can be <u>transferred</u>. This has already been accomplished in the animal world. And to accomplish this on humans is entirely within the realm of possibility . . . within the next 10 years!

One researcher experimented with the inch-long flatworm. Its brain has about 400 cells. They trained the worms to retract into an accordian shape whenever the light went on in their water tank.

The Cannibal Worms

Those worms that were <u>trained</u> to coil upon a light signal were then fed to untrained, cannibal worms. Other cannibal worms were fed <u>un</u>trained flatworms. The cannibal worms that ate trained flatworms exhibited the same reflex behavior when the light was turned on. Memory transfer was working.

Then researchers began working with rats to see if their memories could be transferred to hamsters; thus breaking the species barrier!

They educated the rats and mice to shun darkness. Now rats and mice normally prefer darkness. But they were trained in a reversal technique. Much of this training was done through shock treatments using the Russian Pavlov basic data that was done on dogs many years ago.

Crossing The Species

After the rats and mice were trained, their brains were removed and made into a souplike consistency and injected into hamsters. Soon the injected hamsters began to shun darkness! Memory had been transferred this time across species!

Scientists were further intrigued. What specific substance was the key that triggered the brain to accept transfer of memory? One scientist finally isolated this substance which he called <u>scotophobin</u> (Greek for fear of darkness).

The Peptide Discovery

In further tests some 4000 conditioned rats were killed and their brains were converted to a soupy substance so that an isolation of the triggering molecules could be achieved. What they came up with was <u>peptide</u>. Peptide is a complex amino acid sequence.

Since then several other brain peptides have been discovered.

What are the implications from this research? If these peptides can be synthesized, a large number of *"memories"* can be manufactured as easily as one makes a hammer or nail. Synthesize means that these *"memory banks"* can be created by man without having to extract them from animals. Many more possibilities can be achieved if peptide can be created in the drug laboratories.

Peptide injections could replace school textbooks, as an example. A student would simply receive an injection that would transfer to him the memory of a scholar or genius.

Personality Producers

More sinister, peptide injections could be used to indoctrinate individuals to a passive nature with a *"Casper Milktoast"* personality. A dictator, such as Antichrist, would make much use of a memory exchange bank. He could take the memory of an electronic or space age genius who was uncooperative and inject the memory into

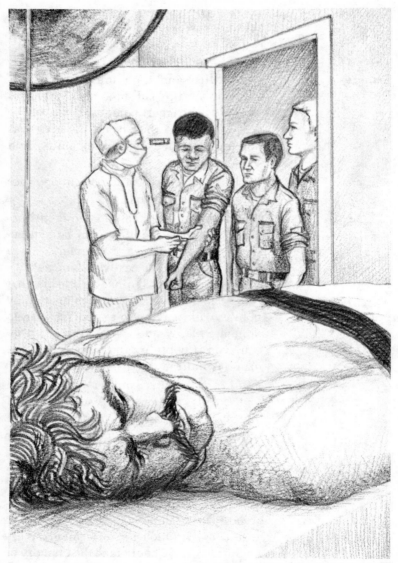

Antichrist, using memory transfer techniques, could order the injection of peptides from murderers and lawless individuals into his entire army to make them aggressive and ruthless.

a cooperative but average intelligent follower.

He could inject peptides of murderers and lawless individuals into his entire army and add a peptide that would give them suicidal tendencies in combat . . . dying without fear for their master.

But there's more!

Not only is it possible to transfer memory . . . but a number of tests have indicated that it is also possible to prevent memory storage!

Memory Erasers

Scientists in using the antibiotic drug called puromycin have been able to actually erase memory in tests with animals.

What a boon this would be in the hands of Antichrist. I often wondered how those living in the Tribulation Period would follow Antichrist and would not want to turn to Christ. Now Scriptures do tell us that they will be under a strong delusion and will believe a lie.

But may it also be possible that Antichrist may exercise a *"memory eraser"* on some uncooperative individuals?

Suppose the Rapture were to occur tomorrow and the Tribulation Period of 7 years were to begin in a month or two. All the people living would have a knowledge of religion. A vast majority of Americans as well as others throughout the world would have a knowledge of the Bible. Millions would remember the evangelistic campaigns of Billy Graham, the television programs of Rex Humbard and Jerry Falwell. There would still be millions of Christian books and Bibles which would reveal exactly what is happening in the Tribulation.

Certainly some, maybe millions would awaken to the fact of their dilemma! And here is where this drug would be useful. Suppose it were administered through the water systems. Or suppose special aircraft were sent aloft to seed the atmosphere.

The Awesome Results

In drinking the water or breathing the air, individuals would unknowingly have certain parts of their memory storage banks erased and their minds would be highly susceptible to new thoughts and ideas.

Highly populated areas such as India could be given an extra dose that would stunt their mental capacities. They would become the menial labor force of the world.

Frightening, isn't it? And it seems untrue. Perhaps right now you are reading this with much skepticism and telling yourself, *"It will never happen!"*

May I suggest you take the time to research the facts, as I have done. Then you will realize why it is so important for us to double our efforts to reaching the lost now . . . and reorganize our priorities.

It is now possible to transfer memories. And it is now possible to erase memories.

And when Antichrist enters the scene, you can be assured he will make use of every devious device to achieve his desired goal of world domination. What are you doing about it . . . right now?

7

BIG BROTHER IS WATCHING YOU

When we think about future events, the coming of Antichrist and the Tribulation Period, we tend to segment these events off as one would view a prophetic chart with vertical bars.

We say we are now living in the Church Age . . . then we place a vertical bar. Next is the Rapture . . . and we place another vertical separating bar. Then comes the Tribulation.

Events Forming Now

Now there is nothing wrong with this thinking, except that the lines are not that definite, in this sense: the events that will take place in the Tribulation Period **are already having their formation right now!**

What we have discussed in previous chapters should open your eyes to this possibility. The sun doesn't set like the drop of an Alka Seltzer tablet - PLOP! The sun begins to set and its brilliant hues paint a picture of real beauty. Gradually, over a period of time, it slowly sinks into the

West as nightfall gradually creeps in, penetrating the light with deep shadows.

Right now, in my opinion, we are in the sunset of this present age. The hues of the sunset are beautiful. Many Christians are experiencing rich blessings in the Lord. Never before has evangelistic work been so prosperous financially and more important, spiritually, in being able to reach millions through modern means of communications.

And yet, creeping through the spectacular sunset are the dreaded darts of night, bringing sinister shades of darkness that reveal utter blackness and hopelessness.

The transfer (outside of the actual Rapture) is gradual . . . almost imperceptive. And even Christians who are dedicated fail to see how close we are to the edge of this darkness and how near we are to the Rapture of the Church!

The events we have discussed in previous chapters are happening now! This is no futuristic scenario. **NOW! NOW! NOW!** And I repeat this three times for emphasis! If you can grasp this and the significance of this statement, your ministry for Jesus Christ should take on a fresh and vibrant acceleration today!

There is no time to waste in large building programs, in self-seeking musicals, in a multitude of non-soul-winning activities that gobble up so much of a church congregation's time. It's time to stop playing

A tiny transmitter could relay a person's movements back to central control . . . and Bible reading in secret could become an impossibility.

Christianity and start working for God with the fervency and dedication of a C. T. Studd, a Jonathan Goforth and a Dwight L. Moody!

Big Brother is <u>already</u> watching you! Particularly if you are accomplishing things for the Lord. I know whereof I speak for I have had personal experiences that have opened my eyes in this matter.

We are living in the age of conformity. By imposing conformity it is far easier to keep track of the population; it is far easier to control them.

A Universal Card

A few years ago the director of the Passport Division of the State Department urged that all Americans be fingerprinted. These fingerprints were to be put on a government identity card. Every citizen would be required to carry one as his personal identification. At this time this has not passed Congress. One day it will!

Already the technology has been developed to attach tiny radio transmitters to the body of any individual. This transmitter would not only keep tabs on the movement of that individual but it could be converted to a transceiver that would also transmit signals. Such signals could control the behavior of that individual!

You Are Being Watched

Many cities already have the <u>Big Eye</u>. These are motion picture cameras mounted on light standards that can zoom and pan and take a close-up photograph of an individual even 200-300 yards away!

The
BIG EAR

Besides the Big Eye, we have the Big Ear! It is no longer necessary to use a bugging device to listen in on conversations. The United States Defense Department has a device that uses a laser beam. The laser beam can be bounced off the window of a room where a conversation is in progress and pick up that conversation!

And all of us are aware of the misuse of computer banks which dip into the private lives of every adult individual in the United States and convert him to a number.

With the complexities of life becoming greater, the Federal Government would like to issue a universal identifier for all Americans. Quite possibly the Social Security number will be the identifying code. When created under Franklin D. Roosevelt, it was never to be used for anything except that singular purpose.

But gradualism has crept in and now the Social Security number is taking on the stigma of The Mark!

A Power
Behind
The Throne

It is natural for one to think that the most powerful force in the United States is the President. And, to a degree, this is true. But a far more awesome and influential force is the C.I.A. (Central Intelligence Agency).

The power of today's C.I.A. is somewhat reminiscent of the Roman Praetorian Guards. The power of the guards was a known and reckoning power, however; while the power of the C.I.A. is cloaked in a garb of secrecy.

The Praetorian Guards were the personal guards of the Roman emperors. They were divided into 9 groups of 1000 men each. Three groups of this highly select task force stayed in Rome to guard the Emperor. They became so powerful they could overthrow emperors whenever they chose.

At Nero's death in 68 A.D., Servius Sulpicius Galba came to Rome intent on becoming the next Emperor. He was a nobleman and had an imposing lineage. But from riotous living his hands and feet were so crooked with gout that he could not wear a shoe or hold a book. Upon becoming Emperor he shocked the army and the populace by running a strict economy and administering justice fairly.

When a senator, Marcus Otho, announced that he could pay his debts only by becoming Emperor, the Praetorian Guards responded with enthusiasm. They declared him Emperor, marched him into the Forum to face Emperor Galba. Galba knew

INTELLIGENCE CONTROL VAST

The **President** of the United States is in direct control of all security and spy operations in the nation. Directly responsible under him in the intelligence pyramid is the **National Security Council** and then the **Director of Central Intelligence.** Under these is a vast network of intelligence divisions which wield a power that no one has been able to fully determine!

Agency	Budget	Employees
C.I.A.	$800 million	20,000
F.B.I.	513 million	20,000
National Security Agency	1.2 billion	24,000
State Department Intelligence	11.5 million	315
Defense Intelligence Agency	200 million	4,300
Military Intelligence	Not available	
Treasury Department Intelligence	926 million	Unavailable
Energy Department Intelligence	24.7 million	Unavailable

he was no match for the guards . . . who promptly cut off his head, his arms, and his lips. Marcus Otho became Emperor!

Both Russia and the United States are masters in the art of gathering intelligence.

One sophisticated method is the formation of spy satellites. It wasn't until a Soviet spy satellite with an atomic reactor re-entered the earth's atmosphere and disintegrated over northwestern Canada that most Americans became aware of the frightening aspects of such a spy network. This event occurred January 24, 1978.

**The
Spy
Satellites**

The star of the U.S. spy satellite stable is the Lockheed "Big Bird." This is a 12-ton technological marvel orbiting as high as 250 miles above the earth. It is equipped with electronic listening equipment along with black-and-white, color and infrared television and still cameras! The exposed film is stored in six cannisters that are periodically ejected into the earth's atmosphere, descend by parachute towards the Pacific Ocean near Hawaii where they are snatched from the air by a giant Y-shaped sky hook bolted to the nose of an Air Force plane.

**No
Hiding
From The
Blackbird**

Along with this the United States has a super plane called the "Blackbird." It's the world's fastest and highest-flying manned aircraft, traveling more than 2000 m.p.h. It can reach 85,000 feet. And it has three-dimensional filming equipment that can cover more than 150 square miles so pre-

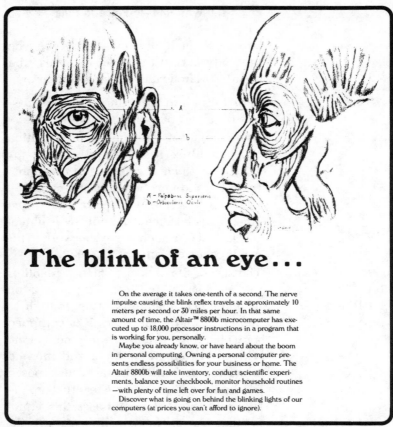

The blink of an eye...

On the average it takes one-tenth of a second. The nerve impulse causing the blink reflex travels at approximately 10 meters per second or 30 miles per hour. In that same amount of time, the Altair™ 8800b microcomputer has executed up to 18,000 processor instructions in a program that is working for you, personally.

Maybe you already know, or have heard about the boom in personal computing. Owning a personal computer presents endless possibilities for your business or home. The Altair 8800b will take inventory, conduct scientific experiments, balance your checkbook, monitor household routines —with plenty of time left over for fun and games.

Discover what is going on behind the blinking lights of our computers (at prices you can't afford to ignore).

This advertisement appeared in a trade magazine for the computer industry. It reveals the efficiency of this particular computer which states that in the blink of an eye (one-tenth of a second) the microcomputer can execute up to 18,000 processor instructions. This is a microcomputer designed for business or home use.

cisely as to locate a mailbox on a country road!

Add to these, laser bugging devices and electronic spy cameras, and you have some idea as to the vastness of the spy system and how difficult it becomes to insure privacy.

Over 100,000 in Intelligence

These techniques are the ones that the Government has allowed us to have some information on. But you can be sure that both the Soviet Union and United States have other devices of spying that are highly classified information . . . information the public may never find out about. And that is frightening to those whose foundation is not in Christ!

Right now you may be watched and not be aware of it! Particularly if you are in any way in the public eye. Pastors who dare to preach the Word of God in its fullness . . . and who begin to influence large segments of the population either in their location or nationwide . . . can be assured of the fact they are being watched and monitored. This is not to say such monitoring is being done by the United States Government; but rather by the forces of evil that would seek to destroy your testimony.

The tools for Antichrist's spy network have already been developed. The stage is set for Big Brother to enter the scene of world dominance.

8

THE SOON COMING BIRTH HATCHERIES

For years now, farmers have developed a superior grade of cattle through selective breeding via sperm banks.

It was over 100 years ago that an Italian researcher discovered that the male sperm could be preserved by freezing. But the technique for this process was only perfected a few years ago; and got underway in a substantial scale in the early 1970's.

With the growing popularity of vasectomies many sperm banks thrived. Today one major U.S. firm is expanding with a large clientele of doctors. It operates from New York City and has several branches.

Code Numbered Babies

Each sperm deposit is assigned a code number. When an order comes in from a doctor for a specific code number, the specimen is shipped in a liquid-oxygen container. Shipments have gone from the United States to all parts of the world. In fact, human babies have been born from sperm frozen for thirteen years.

With this process now a reality it was quite logical that scientists would seek further avenues for *"perfecting"* man.

The next step was *"in vitro fertilization."*

"In vitro" means *"in glass."* And what occurs is that the human egg is fertilized by sperm in a glass tube in a laboratory. The tiny embryo is allowed to grow for a few days. Then it is implanted into the womb of a female. One can visualize the implications of such a procedure. The Russians have conducted extensive studies in this area and at one point had over 200 fetuses growing which had been fertilized in glass test tubes.

Hormones Increase Egg Supply

A male sample may contain 200 million sperm. But usually only one viable egg is released monthly by the female. So scientific minds got together again to resolve this imbalance for their test tube experiments. They developed sex hormones which were introduced into the woman.

The hormones did their work. And as a result, a bumper crop of a dozen or so near-ripe eggs were produced in the ovary. The researcher was able to secure these eggs by making two tiny slits through the woman's abdomen to an ovary. He placed a long, illuminating telescope into one slit. In the other slit went a slender suction device. He then siphoned out several eggs and placed them in laboratory dishes.

Through this technique he could now add donor cells at conception to mold the per-

It would be possible for a husband and wife to purchase an embryo knowing in advance the color of the baby's eyes, hair, its sex and IQ.

sonality and make-up of the future human being.

Choosing Your Embryo

How does this affect you? It is entirely possible that a woman will be able to buy a tiny frozen embryo through her doctor. The doctor will implant this embryo in her uterus. She would carry it for nine months and then give birth to it as though she had conceived it in her own body.

It would be like buying a steam iron with a product guarantee! The embryo would be sold with a guarantee that the resulting baby would be free of genetic defect. In fact, the purchaser would be told in advance the color of the baby's eyes and hair, its sex, its probable size at maturity, and its probable IQ. This prediction would be made by a respected biologist.

As a Christian you would not want this. But, when this becomes possible, millions of women will jump at this opportunity. And what will occur? This will be one further step to break down the sanctity of the individual and the concept of the family as a basic, well-knit unit. It will be another step towards an impersonal numbering system.

Retirement Farms For The Aged

Abortion is now an accepted way of life in America. So, when an in vitro embryo appears defective, it will be a simple matter to wash it down the drain. This will make "retirement farms" more acceptable as well where aged and ill are given a painless death via drugs. The preciousness of

Chinese women are an important part of the work force in Red China. And besides their daily work duties they must participate in military training.

life will give way to the practicality of an efficient society.

Now what is the next step? Yes, there is more!

We now live in a liberated society. More and more women are going out of the home and into the business and industrial world. And in Russia and China, women comprise a major part of the work force. To take nine months out to have a baby cuts productivity and *"encourages individuality."*

The problem: how can we produce babies without sacrificing the time of a woman to incubate the embryo for nine months?

The answer: Place the embryo in an ape or better still, in a cow!

The above is the thinking of Chinese and Russian and some American researchers. Now this does seem way out. But it could become a possibility before the year 2000.

Womb To Womb Transplant

The first step, however, would probably be a *"womb to womb transplant."* A working wife finds out she is pregnant. She wants to have the child but does not want to take the time out in incubation.

A new business would be established. Now not only could you lease cars . . . you could lease wombs for nine months! Mothers are already commanding prices of $10,000 to $20,000 for their babies in the "grey" market. Financially, many women would consider the possibility of leasing their womb.

One embryologist, who has served as an

Will the day come when human embryos are placed in cows for the 9 month gestation period? It is quite possible!

**Human
Babies
in Cows**

advisor to the American Medical Association on reproductive technology examined the possibility of placing the human embryo in the womb of another species. Some reason that since cows have a gestation period of about nine months . . . as do human females they would be a workable choice. Cows don't smoke nor are they given to alcoholism. The birth-giving process is much simpler and less costly.

I know this sounds way out. But this is the type of research going on right now throughout the world. In fact, the Russians hope to give birth to the first totally laboratory-gestated human within a few years, according to one researcher.

Another area of study is to achieve the ability to create a male or female to order according to parent preference. A few years ago, China checked the fetuses of about one hundred women who had recently conceived. They were checked to see how many were male and how many were female. The women were told that 30 of them were carrying female embryos. They elected to have abortions. When the abortions were done, 29 of the aborted embryos were female. Their testing methods were extremely accurate.

**Baby
Hatcheries**

Such experimentation leads to "*baby hatcheries*" where man seeks to manipulate the human form to plasticize it to his mold of uniformity. Genetic scientists will become very popular. And parents may go to a Gene Supermarket before their baby is "*hatched.*"

One well-known geneticist predicts that future societies will regulate who gets born and who does not. The once sacred rights of man will change in many ways. Such a statement recalls the novel I wrote entitled **666** where Faye suffered the consequences of illegally conceiving a child.

What a frightening future awaits those who do not know Jesus Christ as their personal Saviour and Lord.

What may appear to many to be the blessings of progress will in reality become the horrors of hell!

9

BUILDING THE SUPER MAN

Weeding Out Non-Productives

There have been a number of attempts both in the United States and throughout the world to weed out defective humans in an effort to *"improve"* the race.

In Denmark, as an example, sterilization is legally required on all women known to have an IQ under 75. And over 100,000 women in North Carolina have been sterilized over the years because they were termed mentally deficient.

Illinois considered delaying the issuance of marriage licenses on genetic grounds. Vance Packard quotes one of the drafters of the resolution as saying:

> *We are going to have to try to reduce the number of nonproductive members of our society.* [1]

---

[1] Vance Packard, The People Shapers (Boston: Little, Brown and Company) 1977, p. 253.

Hitler was a master in the art of mind manipulation. While he accepted flowers from children, at the same time, multiple thousands of children were being killed methodically in concentration camp gas chambers.

Packard also reveals:

> The challenge is to keep them from falling in love. The biochemist Linus Pauling has proposed a forthright solution.
>
> Small avoidance signals should be tattooed on the forehead of every young carrier [of unwanted genes] [1]

This would begin first on a voluntary basis. But our knowledge of the events that transpire during the Tribulation Period make it evident that such a system would become mandatory, if one wishes to buy or sell!

The Superior Race

Many of us can still recall World War 2 when Hitler issued drastic edicts on sterilization to weed out defectives. And to breed his "superior" race he developed special breeding farms where select girls were given extended privileges for serving the "Fatherland."

Hitler's first move was to remove the undesirables. This was done under the name of

> Charitable Foundation
> for Institutional Care

Killing The Ill

Patients were selected who German doctors felt were unfit for the superior race. The decision became a "State" matter. Neither the victim nor his family were consulted.

In the two years these special euthanasia stations functioned, over 50,000 ill persons were killed by gassing or lethal injec-

---

[1]Vance Packard, The People Shapers (Boston: Little, Brown and Company) 1977, p. 253.

tions. Families were advised of the deaths by a form letter. The letter stated that the patient had died of heart failure or pneumonia. The Nazis cleverly disguised the gas room as a shower bath with seats and douches. It was a sealed room with pipes that carried the deadly gas.

The Devious Code

When Jews discovered the real purpose of the Charitable Foundation for Institutional Care, they no longer let their ill go to the hospital. The Nazis came up with a new name. They identified Jews by codes. The code 14f. 13 became the code that indicated to doctors that the individual would enter a euthanasia center for gassing.

In one camp alone, over one-quarter million Jews perished. A survivor sounded the alarm of what was occurring in a note written to a rabbi. The note concluded:

Creator of the universe, help us!

The sad fact is that initially most Jews refused to believe what was occurring. How could such a thing take place in a civilized society. They discovered it could!

And such inhumanity by man against man will occur again; in greater intensity in the name of science and progress. It's time we wake up!

Hitler wanted to get rid of <u>nonproductive members of society</u>. Now re-read the third paragraph of this chapter. The same phrase is used. How many times have you heard such reasoning, even now! Be aware of the dangers that face us.

Coupled with Hitler's program to eliminate undesirables was an equally agressive program to produce a superior race. To an extent, Russia has employed such techniques.

**Baby
Licenses**

In the January 15, 1971 issue of *BioScience*, Carl Jay Bajema biologist, advanced these ideas for regulating the size of the population:

1. Grant two marketable baby licenses to each family. These would be nonnegotiable.

2. Require married couples who desire children to pass specific tests before they can qualify to have any children.[1]

Those couples who failed to pass the test could then go to the *"human seed bank"* and have a child by *"artifical insemination and/or artificial inovulation."*

**Lock
And
Unlock**

What this becomes is a national parenthood-licensing program. But until that time scientists have been working on long-term contraceptives. One psychologist suggests a Lock/Unlock contraceptive.

All females or males of reproductive age could be required to have this contraceptive capsule inserted into their body. This *"lock"* would prevent their ability to reproduce.

---

[1]Carl Jay Bajema, The Genetic Implications of Population Control, BioScience (January 15, 1971).

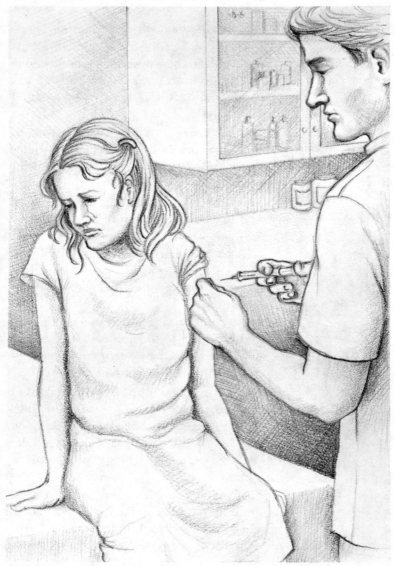

All females or males of reproductive age could be required to have a "lock" capsule inserted into their body to prevent their ability to reproduce.

**Towards
A
Superior
Race**

Upon an approval from the State to have a child, the individual would see his doctor and an antidote would be administered that would unlock his reproductive powers temporarily.

Such steps would be the first in man's desperate attempt to create a superior human race. When will these events occur? Much of these technologies are already possible. The 3-year contraceptive capsule, implanted under the skin, is already here!

When one sees the implications that all this involves, one echoes the plaintive plea of the survivor of a Nazi gas chamber:

Creater of the universe, help us!

10

CREATING THE MONSTER

Cloning

Perhaps nothing is so frightening in duplicating humans as the system called **cloning**.

This is the ultimate in genetic engineering.

> Cloning
> is the production of a new individual
> that has an identical genetic makeup
> to one of the parents.

By taking the nucleus of a mature cell, which has the full number of chromosomes, it is possible to form a zygote[1] that will develop into a replica of the individual from whom the replacement nucleus was taken.

Carbon Copy People

Thus, a mother could produce a child that would be her own identical, but clearly younger, twin (or the identical twin of the father). Or for that matter . . . of another "mother," depending upon where the nucleus for the zygote was taken from.

The cloning technique makes it possible to raise whole families of carbon-copy people

---

[1] Zygote: A cell formed by the union of male and female reproductive cells.

in unlimited numbers — a thousand Einsteins or a thousand Hitlers, etc. One could produce brilliant space scientists or aggressive, rugged soldiers as predictably as stamping out nuts and bolts.

Such techniques are already successfully employed in gardening through the process of grafting. This is how roses are produced on an assembly line basis . . . all identical shades and formation. And genetic engineers are seeking this Utopia for humans.

Rand Corporation scientists estimate that by the year 2005, human cloning will be widespread.

Again millions of people would welcome the opportunity for cloning. It would be a means for them to gain immortality. If you were not a Christian, would you not welcome the opportunity to produce a duplicate copy of YOU, or maybe a triplicate or quadruplicate copy of YOU? Possibly!

The Reasoning

Suppose a child were dying of an incurable disease. Would not many parents jump at the opportunity to create another child <u>exactly identical</u> to the one lost?

So you can see how such genetic engineering will become a desirable boon to those who are self-seeking and without hope.

Cloning opens the way to create a finished man by computer. That is, the computer would analyze *"cell availabilities"* and match up characteristics to produce a desired end product. In cloning, a body cell

Cloning technique make it possible to produce carbon-copy people in unlimited numbers — a thousand Einsteins or a thousand Hitlers! One could produce aggressive soldiers as predictible as stamping out nuts and bolts.

can be taken from just about anywhere in a woman's body, or a man's. That cell would become the master copy cell.

Lets bring this to today's reality. As an example: let's say that today we have too many engineers, too many psychologists and too many teachers creating a surplus market. But we have too few farmers and too few sanitation workers.

The Cloning Committee would issue a decree that for the next two years reproductive cells would be implanted in wombs that would only produce farmers and sanitation workers. Unbelievable? But such a program has already been discussed and is entirely feasible in the future.

Soon Coming Reality

Again the Rand Corporation, a research organization with many scientists on its advisory staff, suggests that specialized human mutants could become a reality by the year 2025!

What bag of worms does cloning unleash?

With a *"cloned individual"* it will become easy for a computer to keep track of him and to even read his thoughts and his intents . . . before he takes a course of action! And, upon this read-out, the computer could be programmed to redirect his actions and his thoughts! What a tool in the hands of an Antichrist!

Also advances could be made in modern medicine for a Uniform Spare Parts Division. Since cloned individuals become identical, there would be less rejection of

Human engineers ponder the once and future man

The plight of the individual in the f... onrushing technol... more ... within ... person ... alter h... manize ... genes, t... will eve... tionary ... man. It w... fantastic ... "better" p... and anim... menial ch... Living but ... only to be ... plants are a...

The implic... and society ... has man act... the chance to ... moral and phi... that opportun... alarming pauci... how—indeed, i... ing technologies ...

Vance Packa... deserves to be r... pulls together c... stand reports on ...

The People Shap...
by Vance Packard
Little, Brown • 398

shaping frontiers b... temporary science. ... ture, at once inspiri... should help to organi... that is sorely needed.

Lacking outside ... guidelines such as th... tarily by genetic engi...rs for research on mutated bacteria, some people-shaping methods are creeping out of the laboratory and into daily life. For example, Packard reports that last year between 10% and 20% of the public school teachers on the East Coast were systematically practicing behavior modification techniques in their classrooms—mainly sophisticated conditioned-reflex methods. There is no indication that the teachers obtained the prior consent of the parents concerned, or that the students were made aware that they were being manipulated.

Similar covert efforts to manipulate masses of people are discussed in several chapters in the first part of the book, which examines the history of, and the latest developments in, techniques for

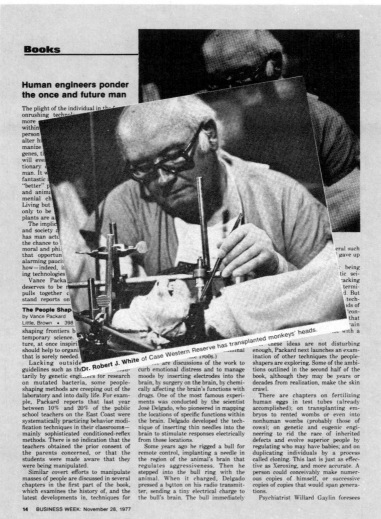

Dr. Robert J. White of Case Western Reserve has transplanted monkeys' heads.

...e 1960s.) ...are discussions of the work to curb emotional distress and to manage moods by inserting electrodes into the brain, by surgery on the brain, by chemically affecting the brain's functions with drugs. One of the most famous experiments was conducted by the scientist José Delgado, who pioneered in mapping the locations of specific functions within the brain. Delgado developed the technique of inserting thin needles into the brain to stimulate responses electrically from those locations.

Some years ago he rigged a bull for remote control, implanting a needle in the region of the animal's brain that regulates aggressiveness. Then he stepped into the bull ring with the animal. When it charged, Delgado pressed a button on his radio transmitter, sending a tiny electrical charge to the bull's brain. The bull immediately

...eral such ...gave up ...being ...tic sei-...acking ...termi-...d. But ...tech-...ds of ...con-...that ...ain ...with a

...inal

...nese ideas are not disturbing enough, Packard next launches an examination of other techniques the people-shapers are exploring. Some of the ambitions outlined in the second half of the book, although they may be years or decades from realization, make the skin crawl.

There are chapters on fertilizing human eggs in test tubes (already accomplished); on transplanting embryos to rented wombs or even into nonhuman wombs (probably those of cows); on genetic and eugenic engineering to rid the race of inherited defects and evolve superior people by regulating who may have babies; and on duplicating individuals by a process called cloning. This last is just as effective as Xeroxing, and more accurate. A person could conceivably make numerous copies of himself, or successive copies of copies that would span generations.

Psychiatrist Willard Gaylin foresees

This full page review of the excellent book, *The People Shapers* by Vance Packard, appeared in Business Week magazine. Inset photo reveals that experiments have already been conducted on transplanting monkey heads.

a foreign implant such as a new kidney or a new heart.

Brain Transplants

But there's more. Right now in a Cleveland clinic, experiments are in progress in transplanting live brains! One professor of neurosurgery concluded that the best way to transplant a brain was to transfer an entire head! This is vastly more simple.

Head Transplants

To switch heads, it is only necessary to sever a few connecting muscles and vessels and then unite them to the neck of the headless recipient body! Because the words "head transplant" are so repugnant to society today, it is called a "cephalic transplant." Cephalic means head.

The brain is one of the easiest of all organs to transplant! Both in the United States and in Russia, head transplants have been done successfully . . . on animals! This has been going on since 1970! Monkeys with transplanted heads accept and chew food. The monkeys make their usual monkey sounds and their eyes follow you as you move throughout the room.

Scientists have reported that unlike transplanting other organs, they have never seen a brain transplant rejected on the new animal.

What are the implications of this . . . prophetically?

You may recall that Antichrist, during the final 3½ years of the Tribulation (known as the Great Tribulation), is allowed by God's permissive will to achieve some sort of universal domination.

Antichrist
Slain and
Healed

He is permitted to persecute the saints
(Revelation 12). The mass of humanity will
follow Antichrist. And the worship of
Antichrist will for that day and age consti-
tute the worship of the one behind him,
Satan, the Dragon.

We are told in Revelation 13:3:

And I saw one of the heads
as if it had been slain,
and his fatal wound was healed.
And the whole earth was amazed
and followed after the beast [Antichrist].

The fatal wound of the head may be something that befalls the Antichrist as an individual as the leader of the then dominant
European head of the final Satanic government. Is Antichrist assassinated?
Reading Revelation 13:11, 12, and 14 sheds
further light:

And I saw another beast [The False Prophet]
coming up out of the earth;
and he had two horns like a lamb,
and he spoke as a dragon.

And he exercises all the authority
of the first beast [Antichrist]
in his presence.
And he makes the earth
and those who dwell in it
to worship the first beast,
whose fatal wound was healed.

And he deceives those
who dwell on the earth . . . the
telling those who dwell on earth
to make an image to the beast
who had the wound of the sword
and has come to life.

Scriptures seem to indicate that Antichrist will be killed and apparently by a sword. We do know that execution in some Middle East countries is achieved by cutting off one's head with a sword. This still goes on.

**Is This
The
Answer?**

Could perhaps some assassin whip out a sword and decapitate Antichrist? Or, on the other hand, could Antichrist receive a fatal wound on his body, which became irreparable? And, therefore, could his head be severed surgically and transplanted on the body of a young man?

We don't know. But such is a possibility, particularly in light of what we have just discussed on cloning and head transplants.

Suddenly those things in Revelation which many thought were unbelievable and symbolic, in light of today's advances, become altogether plausible and possible.

We are now living in the age of the capability of producing a super man, a monster.

That monster will be Antichrist!

The first 10 chapters have shown how man is being manipulated for eventual end-time control by Antichrist.

The remaining chapters show how the Middle East will become the focal point of world politics and how Antichrist will manipulate and control nations.

11

THE TRANSITION TO TERROR

Roses Bloom In Israel!

In Israel, the desert is blossoming as a rose. Last winter Israel sold 50 million roses to Europe. The flowers are cheaper than those grown in America or Europe, in spite of shipping costs.

Both fruits and flowers from Israel are shipped daily on jumbo jets to all points of the world. We are reminded of the Scripture:

> The wilderness and the dry land
> shall be glad,
> the desert shall rejoice
> and blossom as the rose
> and the autumn crocus.
> It shall blossom abundantly. . . .
> (Isaiah 35:1,2 Amplified)

These verses refer, of course, to the 1000 year Millennium when Israel will be regathered and there will be economic prosperity, freedom from oppression, unified worship and a world at peace.

Right now we are witnessing an imitation prototype of things to come. In the last few

It took over 3000 years to accomplish. But on November 25, 1977 President Anwar Sadat landed on Israeli soil to be met by Prime Minister Menahem Begin. This was the first such political meeting since Moses confronted Pharaoh!

**We Are
Witnessing
A Pattern
of
Things To Come**

years seven kingdoms on the Persian Gulf have emerged as a modern marvel. They are called the United Arab Emirates. Brian Silk, in the London Telegraph described this awakening in the Middle East as follows:

> A land of superlatives and records where the money pours like a seemingly inexhaustible spring which washes away the sand dunes and turns them to concrete and asphalt.

Abu Dhabi is now the richest spot on earth with an annual per capita income of $22,000! The Middle East is fast becoming the geopolitical center of the earth.

**28 Minutes
in
3000 Years**

It was just a 28-minute jet flight from an air base in Egypt to Tel Aviv's Ben Gurion airport. But it took over 3000 years to accomplish! On November 25, 1977 the most dramatic political confrontation occurred that has ever taken place in the Middle East since Moses confronted Pharaoh!

President Anwar Sadat of Egypt met in peace negotiations with Prime Minister Menahem Begin of Israel . . . on Israeli soil! This historic meeting was watched live via satellite by television viewers worldwide! It was an historic meeting that many hoped would reconcile the descendants of Jacob and Ishmael.

The Sadat visit to Jerusalem broke down the barrier between Arab and Jew. No major foreign diplomat had ever before spoken before the Knesset (Israeli Parliament) . . . not even the President of the

United States. That privilege was reserved for Israel's arch enemy.

Christians the world over began to ask questions. How does this event tie in with Bible prophecy? Again, what we are seeing is an imitation of the real thing. There will be no peace in the Middle East until the Prince of Peace breaks the bonds of sin in His dramatic appearance at the Battle of Armageddon, at the end of the 7-year Tribulation Period.

Arab and Jew may settle for a peace now . . . but, if they do, it will only be a temporary period and a semblance of peace, rather than real peace. What we witnessed at this historic meeting was simply a cooling off period. But it will generate into greater bitterness and war!

The First Time Since Moses

Further news was made when Prime Minister Menahem Begin of Israel flew to Egypt on Christmas Day, 1977 to continue peace talks. For the first time since Moses, an Israeli leader, Prime Minister Begin, visited Egypt. And both nations issued a call to the United States to help them in their negotiations. Then, on January 12, 1978, Foreign Minister Moshe Dayan of Israel met with Pope Paul VI in Rome to discuss the future of Jerusalem and peace moves in the Middle East.

Now can you see the parallels developing that are becoming a prototype of what will occur during the Tribulation Period. Let me define them for you further.

During the Tribulation Period:

The Threat of Extinction

1. Israel will experience the harassment of the nations of the world.

2. She will have experienced the threat of extinction by an invasion attempt by Russia and her satellites (probably North and South African nations, Eastern Europe and Iran). A protest will be made but will go unheeded (Ezekiel 38:13).

   Russia and her armies are destroyed on the mountains of Israel as a result of divine intervention (Ezekiel 39:2-4).

3. Antichrist and his armies (The European Confederacy) will come to the defense of Israel as her protector (Daniel 11:40b-45).

4. The protector will become the persecutor during the Great Tribulation known as the Abomination of Desolation (Daniel 12:11).

5. The religious world leader (the False Prophet) will deceive millions with his counterfeit religion.

Let's review this briefly. What is happening right now?

1. Russia is the enemy of Israel.

2. The Arab nations are the enemy of Israel.

3. Israel faces the threat of extinction.

4. Sadat, an Arab leader, initiates peace moves with Israel.

On January 12, 1978, Israeli Foreign Minister Moshe Dayan meets with Pope Paul VI in the papal private study for consultation on world affairs.

On February 13, 1978, Egyptian President Anwar Sadat meets with Pope Paul VI in the papal private study for consultation on world affairs.

5. The peace moves flounder.

6. Both Israel and Egypt call on the United States for support and instruction.

7. Foreign Minister Moshe Dayan of Israel calls on Pope Paul VI for guidance on Jerusalem.

8. The United States takes an active part in the Middle East, controlling the actions of Israel and *"talking peace."*

Parallels in Prophecy

Can you see the parallels? What is occurring now is actually a pattern of what will occur during the Tribulation Period. Never before have we seen such a well-defined pattern to End-Time prophecy!

Now, let's look behind the scenes of this transition to terror.

Right now the United States must increase its defense building by $56 billion during the next five years in order to keep pace with the Soviet Union. The Soviet Union advances in satellite-destroying weapons leave the U.S. with little choice but to get into the space weapon race with the U.S.S.R.

Weapons of War

Coupled with this is the U.S. sale of arms to nonallied countries in 1979 alone which will total close to $10 billion! American sales of military equipment to all nations is over $13 billion annually!

With the race neck-to-neck in weapons of war, Western intelligence sources now reveal that the Soviet Union is believed to be breeding new strains of killer viruses and

Era of Bionic Person Moves Nearer to Reality

Medical engineers are coming up with more and more electronic aids for the crippled, deaf, mute and blind. Devices promise added powers to the able-bodied, too.

The 6-million-dollar bionic man or woman of fiction, put together with plastic, metal and electronic parts, is getting closer to reality.

Researchers and medical engineers are devising replacements for the human body—from skin to spinal cord—holding out the promise of finding ways to permit the ░░░ the deaf ░░░ the blind ░░░ capped p░░░

The ad░░░ vate and ░░░ througho░░░ around the ░░░

Many of ░░░ vantage o░░░ compress ░░░ complicate░░░ small units░░░ can fit on ░░░ computer l░░░ roomful of e░░░

Some of th░░░ bionics is in ░░░ Hundreds of ░░░ ted with m░░░ arms, with ░░░ hands that ░░░ close via br░░░ The secret: S░░░ trodes pick up ░░░ pulses, which ░░░ magnified a t░░░ times by a pow░░░ and transmitted ░░░ iature motors in ░░░ chanical hand.

Early models ░░░ bionic arms are ░░░ and limited to ░░░ with below-elbo░░░ putations. Sturdi░░░ sions are to in░░░ mind-operated e░░░ and wrists.

Artificial skin, a ░░░ off from plastics us░░░ spacecraft, now is b░░░ placed over transdu░░░ and integrated-contro░░░ mechanisms to give a ░░░ sense of touch to ampu░░░ tees. The aim is to en░░░ able a person with a ░░░ replacement hand to lift ░░░ a glass without crushing ░░░ it or dropping it.

Similar sensors in the heels of artificial and paralyzed legs can send feedback messages to the crippled to assure firm footing.

Humanlike voice. For those who cannot speak, hand-held voice synthe sizers are available. ░░░

places, including the Institute for Biomedical Engineering at the University of Utah, Columbia-Presbyterian Medical Center in New York City, the University of Florida at Gainesville, and in Canada. The basic approach is this:

Television cameras direct signals to a computer, which relays them through wires to the brain. Blind volunteers using such devices to scan pages in which letters are represented by Braille dots have been able to read much faster than they did with their finger tips.

Scientists now are concentrating on the tough job of ░locating the proper ░░░ which various sig░░░. They foresee the ░░ when a tiny TV ░░plated in an eye ░ of the system— ░░ocessor, transmit- ░compressed into ░░.

░░ancisco are work- ░stem, which con- ░es that can be ░nd. A small TV ░eyeglasses picks ░ the wearer and ░lastic garment ░abdomen. The ░ as patterns of ░eels. ░erimenters say ░kly learned to ░ identify com- ░phones, drink- ░, chairs and ░.

░ devices al- ░ being used ░ to allow the ░ct things by ░ther senses ░aring and ░ial canes, ░spectacles ░le for the ░ objects— ░ne poles, ░branches ░ as a bat ░nals sent ░ devices ░rom the ░e vibra- ░an hear ░r feel.

By means of various pitches and intensities, some devices indicate how far away an object is, in which direction it lies, its size and its roughness.

For the blind, new reading machines with optical sensors scan pages, converting print-

The Electronic Body Ahead
Research under way—

Eyes—combined tiny TV cameras, computers that enable blind to "see"

Hands, arms—today's artificial limbs that move in response to thoughts

Internal organs—nuclear power packs that trim size of manufactured organs

Muscles—synthetic muscle activated by sound and magnets

Hearing—sensor implants that bypass diseased nerves

Voice—today's hand-held synthesizers that fuse sounds into words

Spinal cord—electrical "bridges" spanning damage to nervous system

Skin—plastic skin, sensors that give "touch" to new heels, fingers

The above news article appeared in *U.S. News & World Report*. Almost all major parts of the body can now be replaced with plastic, metal or electronic devices. It is estimated that an artificial heart will be perfected in the next 5 years. Inset indicates research on planning an electronic body.

microbes in heavily guarded biological warfare factories.

And in both countries, the U.S. and Russia, scientists have created an artificial gene that, like a tiny robot, acting on orders, can make an exact copy of a human brain hormone.

Freak Weather Patterns Suspicious

During January and February, 1978, the United States suffered severe weather disasters. It was termed a "freak of nature." But it has been known that the most active weather alteration research is now being conducted in the Soviet Union.

The East Coast was devastated by snow storms in January and February, 1978. February 5-6 were black days for New England. It was the worst winter storm in New England's history and virtually shut down all activity. To give you an idea of how crippling such a storm pattern can be, the city of Philadelphia alone spend over $1.5 million in two days just for snow removal!

These storms followed mysterious blasts that occurred off the East Coast of the U.S. in November and December, 1977.

It is quite evident we are seeing a pattern develop that points to the increasing persecution of the people of Israel and the ensuing holocaust of Armageddon.

The Long Road To Israel

The people of Israel have yet to acknowledge Jesus Christ as their Messiah. They are still trying to take on a Goliath in their own strength. They are still scattered over all the world.

The majority of the Jewish population is situated as follows:

1. United States   5.7 million
2. Israel   3.1 million
3. Soviet Union   2.6 million

The world Jewish population is approximately 14.3 million of which almost 12 million are concentrated in three countries!

Slowly, but surely, this 12 million will begin their pilgrimage back to their homeland, Israel.

When this occurs, it will begin the transition to terror!

12

RUSSIA'S RISE TO RUIN

**How
Antichrist
Comes into
Power**

Either at sometime **prior to the Rapture** of believers or **during the first 3 1/2 years** of the 7-year Tribulation Period, Russia will take an interest in Israel's wealth.

Why would Russia want Israel?

Perhaps the great prize which Russia wants is the vast mineral deposits in the Dead Sea. The Dead Sea is 1286 feet below sea level, the lowest spot on the surface of the earth! It is 50 miles long and nine miles wide. It is still known as the "Sea of Salt" because it is filled with salt due to its having no outlet. Fed chiefly by the Jordan River, its waters have evaporated for thousands of years in the fiery heat, leaving behind an ever-growing residue of salt and other valuable minerals. It is calculated that there is enough potash in the Dead Sea to provide the needs of the entire world for 2000 years!

With a growing famine in the world, potash becomes extremely important since

As the world edges on the brink of famine, major nations will focus their attention on the prized Dead Sea because it is a rich source of fertilizer. Russia may also seek this valuable potash deposit for making explosives.

it is used as fertilizer. Vegetation, and consequently animal life including human life desperately require it!

But potash also has another use; that is in the making of explosives.

Russia Occupies 1/6th of Land Surface

Russia — the Union of Soviet Socialist Republics — in area the largest country in the world — stretches across two continents from the North Pacific to the Baltic Sea. It occupies 1/6th of the earth's land surface.

So Russia, with her allies, will according to the Scriptures someday invade Israel (Ezekiel 38:1-39:16). At this time, because of Russia's march against the comparatively defenseless Jews, God's wrath is kindled:

> And it shall come to pass at the same time when Gog [Russia] shall come against the land of Israel, saith the Lord Jehovah, that My wrath shall come up into My nostrils.
> (Ezekiel 38:18)

God Brings Judgment

The heavens will open and God will pour out a judgment from heaven that will wipe out the Russian military might and much of the power of the Russian confederacy. What judgments are they?

There will be a severe earthquake and the earth around Israel will tremble severely. This earthquake will throw the soldiers into such a panic that in confusion they will kill one another.

> . . . the mountains will be thrown down . . . every wall will fall to the ground.

> Every man's sword will be against his brother. (Ezekiel 38:20-21)

In addition to this, sudden calamities will strike them and very violent rain and hail will fall down on them. And if this were not enough — fire and brimstone will explode right in their very midst. See Ezekiel 38:22.

Through this righteous indignation of God, we will find that the Russian armies with their allies will be destroyed without even being attacked by any other nations. All but one-sixth of the army will be killed! See Ezekiel 39:2.

What is the extent of this vast judgment?

> Then those who inhabit the cities of Israel will go out, and make fires with the weapons and burn them, both shields and bucklers, bows and arrows, war clubs and spears and for seven years, they will make fires of them ... For seven months the house of Israel will be burying them ... Even all the people of the land will bury them.
>
> (Ezekiel 39:9, 12, 13)

7 Months to Bury the Dead

It takes 7 years to burn and destroy weapons and 7 months to bury the dead. So great are the casualties that it takes all of the people of Israel to help in this great task!

With this destruction of much of the Russian power, a power vacuum is created. And Antichrist rushes in to close this vacuum!

In attempting to settle the Arab-Israeli dispute, he will side with Israel and back her claim to the land of Palestine against Russia.

**Russia Backs
Arab's Claim**

Russia will back the Arabs' claim to Palestine (Ezekiel 38).

Because the Antichrist will make a pledge to protect Israel the Jews will no doubt flock back to Israel in unprecedented numbers.

The Scriptures seem to give us some indication that in this time Russia may part with her Jews and allow them to return to Israel. It is estimated that there are over 2 million Jews in Russia at present.

After this occurs, Russia, feeling she is all powerful, will probably make her move into the land of Israel.

God will allow this to happen because He will not tolerate His people looking to the Antichrist as their saviour. Therefore, the Jews will again be driven out of their land and many will flee from Israel and the two thirds of those left behind will be slain so that, alas, the soil of Israel will again be drenched with the blood of the children of Abraham.

And it shall come to pass, that in all the land, saith the Lord, two parts therein shall be cut off and die; but the third shall be left therein (Zechariah 13:8).

And among these nations shalt thou find no ease, neither shall the sole of thy foot have rest: but the Lord shall give thee there a trembling heart, and failing of eyes, and sorrow of mind: (65)

And thy life shall hang in doubt before thee; and thou shalt fear day and night, and shalt have none assurance of thy life: (66)

In the morning thou shalt say, Would God it were even! and at even thou shalt say, Would God it were morning! for the fear of thine heart wherewith thou shalt fear, and for the sight of thine eyes which thou shalt see (67) (Deuteronomy 28:65-67).

God Steps In

After this occurs may be the time when God will step in and devastate Russia and Russian Communism, including her allies as He has prophesied in Ezekiel 38:1-39:16.

It seems that this is the time that the Federated States of Russia will back the Arabs' claim to Palestine (Ezekiel 38).

Russia's Final Day

This may be the time that the Federated States of Europe will move into this vacuum created by the defeat of Russia. It is at this time that Antichrist will rule over all the earth.

RUSSIAN POWER TO GROW . . .

The two superpowers—the Soviet Union and the United States—account for 10% of the world's population.

The Soviet Union now has over 275 million people and the United States trails with 220 million. One day Russia will fall in judgment as it attempts to erase Israel from the map. Then Antichrist will move in and attempt to control the entire world.

By the year 2000, the world's population will be over 8 billion people. It is important to remember that China's population of almost 900 million is rising by 14 million a year. It will easily top one billion by the year 2000. China, with Japan, will comprise the bulk of the Asian army that will seek to overthrow the forces of Antichrist in the latter part of the 7-year Tribulation Period.

More than half of the world's population lives in Asia (57%). While only 10.2% live in Europe. Should Antichrist reign in the year 2000 he would control over 8 billion people.

No one knows when Antichrist will emerge! We do know, however, that we stand at the threshold of this tragic event . . . and that we are now witnessing the climate that will usher in the rise of Antichrist!

13

THE RISE OF ISRAEL'S MOST VICIOUS PERSECUTOR

**The
Peace Mission
Had Failed**

Three top Israeli leaders and Secretary of State Henry A. Kissinger faced each other behind the closed doors of the prime minister's office in Jerusalem.

The time was late Saturday night, March 22, 1975.

Yigal Allon, Israeli Foreign Minister, turned to Kissinger to say that he expected the secretary back in the Middle East in two or three weeks.

Allon was an old friend of Kissinger. And it was in sadness that Henry Kissinger had to tell his friend that this peace mission had failed. In fact, personal shuttle diplomacy seemed to have reached an end . . . the negotiations between Israel and Egypt had been shattered!

Later that same evening, in the privacy of Kissinger's King David hotel room, Shimon Peres, Israeli Defense Minister, broke down into tears.

It was a dramatic moment when the full

weight of the consequences hit these leaders as they realized that the failure of this mission again meant an uncertain future for the Middle East.

At the airport, Henry Kissinger held back the tears. His voice trembled as he said that it was a sad day for Israel and for the United States.

Henry Kissinger had staked his reputation and that of the United States on this two-week shuttle diplomacy. His mistake was in believing he could move either Egypt or Israel from a standstill position.

Anwar Sadat, the Egyptian President, was not willing to meet certain Israeli demands. And the Israeli's were not willing to cede territorial conquests.

Israel had fought four wars since 1948. And all they had to show for it were meaningless "pieces of paper" that each time ultimately led to yet another war.

The next step was the Geneva Conference where the Soviet leadership would have a hand in attempting a settlement. And this would be the beginning of the end!

Jewish Group Opposes Zionism

And even while these negotiations were going on, a small group of orthodox Jews based in Jerusalem, were quickly opening their own lines of communication with the Palestine Liberation Organization (PLO).

The Watchers of the City (**Neturei Karta**, in Hebrew), rather surprisingly, share the PLO's opposition to Zionism, but for quite another reason.

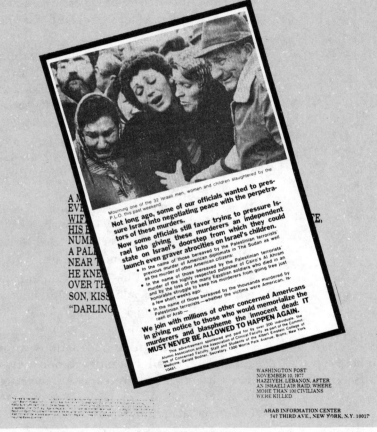
The tragedy of the Middle East wars is the loss of life of innocent bystanders. Both the Palestinians and the Israelis have been responsible for deaths of civilians . . . including little children. Both of these ads (by Palestinians and Israelis) picture atrocities and seek public support. Both appeared in the same issue of *The New York Times*.

HOW TO IDENTIFY ANTICHRIST

(A Comparative Study of Daniel and Revelation)

To get some insight on the rise of Antichrist, let us look at some descriptive verses in both the prophetic books of Daniel (in the Old Testament) and Revelation (in the New Testament).

... behold, a fourth beast, dreadful and terrifying and extremely strong; and it had large iron teeth.

It devoured and crushed, and trampled down the remainder with its feet; and it was different from all the beasts that were before it, and it had ten horns.

As for the ten horns, out of this kingdom ten kings will arise; and another will arise after them, and he will be different from the previous ones, and will subdue three kings.

(Daniel 7:7, 24)

And I stood upon the sand of the seashore. And I saw a beast coming up out of the sea, having ten horns and seven heads, and on his horns were ten diadems, and on his heads were blasphemous names.

And the ten horns which you saw are ten kings, who have not yet received a kingdom, but they receive authority as kings with the beast for one hour.

These have one purpose and they give their power and authority to the beast.

(Revelation 13:1; 17:12, 13)

A COMPARISON BETWEEN DANIEL'S FOURTH BEAST
AND THE BEAST OF REVELATION

Daniel's Fourth Beast:	Revelation's Beast:	
Comes up out of the sea (7:3)	Comes up out of the sea (13:1)	
	Seven heads (13:1)	
Ten horns—ten kings (7:7, 24)	Ten horns—ten kings (13:1; 17:12)	
Another horn (Antichrist) becomes dominant ruler (7:24-26)	The beast as a person (cf. 19:20) becomes dominant ruler (17:12-13)	
	Like a leopard (13:2)	This beast has characteristics from each of
Stamped with the feet (7:7)	Feet of a bear (13:2)	Daniel's first three beasts viz., lion,
Great iron teeth (7:7)	Mouth of a lion (13:2)	bear & leopard (Daniel 7:4-6).
	Scarlet color (17:3)	
Blasphemous (7:25)	Blasphemous (13:5)	
	Dragon gives him power (13:2)	
Persecutes saints (7:21)	Persecutes saints (13:7; 11:7)	
Power for a time, times, and a dividing of a time (1 + 2 + 1/2 = 3 1/2 years) (7:25)	Power for 42 months (3 1/2 years) (13:5)	
Defeated by God who then sets up the Kingdom (7:21-22, 26-27)	Defeated by God who then sets up the Kingdom (19:11; 20:6)	

Let's examine the Scripture verses just quoted. The sea, as in the similar case of Daniel 7:2-3, refers to the sea of nations which is troubled like an ocean with roaring and crashing waves—as empires rise and fall. So, too, in Revelation 17:15, the *"waters"* of the sea are explicitly declared to be nations and peoples.

In Daniel 7 and 8 various *"beasts,"* wild-animals, proved to be great empires often headed by certain individuals. And the horns atop the beasts represented various notable kings of that empire. In fact, both Daniel 7:24 and Revelation 17:12, tell us plainly that the horns represent kings.

Thus here in Revelation 13:1 John is seeing an end-time empire rise up out of the political struggles amid the nations. As we, too, see it ascend out of the waters we stand amazed—for it is an empire that we have seen before in the past prophetic visions of the Scriptures! It is the Fourth Beast of Daniel 7 (Daniel 7:7-8, 19-28).

There is a special chart in this section entitled, <u>A Comparison Between Daniel's Fourth Beast and the Beast of Revelation.</u> It would be wise for you to look at this chart now.

Daniel 7's Fourth Beast was the Roman Empire which was seen to linger in the world in some way until the time of Christ's Second Coming (Daniel 7:23-27). So likewise, this Beast of Revelation lingers until it is destroyed by Christ at His coming at the end of the Tribulation at the

The Image of Daniel 2

606 ± B.C.
Gold — Nebuchadnezzar's
Babylon (Unquestioned
obedience to one absolute
sovereign)

536 ± B.C.
Silver — The dual Empire of
the Medes & Persians
(The 2 arms!)

336 B.C.
Copper — The Greek
Empire

200 ± B.C.
Iron Legs United —
Roman Republic & Empire

300 ± A.D.
Iron Legs Divided —
Western & Eastern
Roman Empire

476 & 1453 A.D. (They fall)

Iron Legs Cracking —
European States

Iron & Clay Feet — End-time
Lawlessness (Communism)?

10 Toes — Revived Rome
Confederacy

A.D.?

A-4

Battle of Armageddon (Revelation 19:19-20).

Thus clearly this Beast of Revelation must be the final manifestation of the Roman Empire which will be in the world at the times of the end. Thus some have called it the *"Revived Roman Empire.'* (Students of prophecy who have studied Daniel 2 will also realize that this chapter too shows that the Roman Empire will in some sense survive until Christ comes. The iron which represents Rome, in Daniel 2, lasts until the end—although it becomes mixed with clay.)

End-time Europe

But someone asks, *"Didn't the Roman Empire fall away? Then how can it be in existence at the end when Christ comes?"* Answer: Yes, it did fall away in name; but its constituents, the European nations which made it up still linger in the cracked up divided continent of Europe. In fact, Daniel 2 pictures the Roman Empire—the iron in the image of Daniel 2—as being eventually divided into two legs (the E and W empires, divided by Emperor Diocletian in 300 A.D.) and then later cracking into pieces (into the present divided Europe)! Thus this Beast represents the final state that Europe and the Mediterranean world will be in during the end-times.

It is definitely the **final** manifestation of this empire as it, the Beast, meets its end at Christ's Armageddon coming (Revelation 19:19-21). Its period of power and persecution is brief, *"one hour"* (Revelation

Israeli soldiers remain on constant alert even while praying at the Wailing Wall in Jerusalem. In the beginning of the Tribulation Period Antichrist will gain Israel's confidence and lull her into relaxing her military preparedness. This will be Israel's tragic error!

17:12)—that is, the 42 months (3 1/2 years) which make up the awful last half of the Tribulation Period (Revelation 13:5).

10 Confederate Rulers

This end-time wicked empire will be some sort of a confederation of 10 rulers, "kings." Here Revelation 13:1 shows them as horns as does Daniel 7:7, 24, while Daniel 2:41-44 portrays them as the toes of Nebuchadnezzar's dream-image. It is these toes which the rock, Christ, strikes at His Armageddon Coming (Daniel 2:34, 44).

Revelation 17:12-13 shows us plainly that the 10 horns will in some manner form a coalition, and together give their power to the Beast. Thus we await a time when the European nations will band together into some type of 10 nation confederacy—and in this way **revive the Roman Empire!** Is the present European Common Market the precursor of this coming empire?

Antichrist Will Arise

Here read Daniel 7:8, 20-21, 24-28. These verses show that another leader will arise, and this new horn will be victorious in a power struggle with three of the kings.

Then this new horn will blaspheme God and persecute the saints intensely for 3 1/2 years. **This 11th horn is the Antichrist!** It is he who will commit the Abomination of Desolation in the rebuilt Jerusalem temple (2 Thessalonians 2:3-4; Matthew 24:15). It is he who will lead the armies to Armageddon on some diabolical mission—and here he will be cast directly into the Lake of Fire by Christ (Revelation 19:19-21).

Since this 11th horn, the Antichrist, is shown to be the persecutor of the Tribulation Saints during the final 3 1/2 years of the Tribulation (Daniel 7:20-28) it is seen that THIS 11TH HORN OF DANIEL, THE ANTICHRIST, AND THE ENTIRE BEAST OF REVELATION DO THE **SAME** THINGS (Revelation 13:4-7); AND LIKEWISE BOTH PERISH AT THE COMING OF CHRIST AT ARMAGEDDON TO ESTABLISH HIS KINGDOM.

Why? **Answer:** The 11th horn, the Antichrist, when he becomes the leader of the ten nation Mediterranean-European Confederation, asserts his will over the entire BEAST empire, so that the mind of the Antichrist (the person; the 11th horn) becomes synonymous with the mind of the entire evil Beast empire.

It is this relationship which the Antichrist as a person has to the Beast-empire which he dominates (as Christ will someday dominate His Kingdom) that explains why the Beast of Revelation seems to be at the same time a person and a nation!

Thus the Beast is an end-time empire as the animals in Daniel 7 are empires; but the Beast is also a person who is cast at the end into the Lake of Fire at Christ's coming (Revelation 19:19-21; and here the Beast *cannot* be the entire empire, for the army part of the empire, merely die and go to Hades while the Beast goes directly to the Lake of Fire).

In this same way in Daniel 2:38, the golden

head of the image stood both for the nation Babylon and at the same time for its notable king, Nebuchadnezzar. So, too, it was said of Adolf Hitler *"Der Furhrer ist Deutschland and Deutschland ist der Fuhrer,"* or "The Leader (Hitler) is Germany and Germany is the Leader (Hitler)." Hitler was introduced this way in a great rally in the late 1930's. So, too, will the BEAST be the final European-Mediterranean Confederacy as well as its supreme evil mind and leader, the 11th horn dictator, the Antichrist!

7 Heads Represent World Dominion

The heads? In Daniel 7:6 the beast representing the Greek Empire's period of domination had FOUR HEADS, one head for each of the four geographical sections of the post-Alexander the Great Greek Empire. After Alexander had made his conquests and died (336-323 B.C.) his empire was divided into four regions by his generals, and with slight adjustments this was the status quo until the rise of Rome.

If the heads of this Beast of Revelation are interpreted similarly, then the **7 heads** must represent geographical regions. The fact that there are SEVEN heads, the number used everywhere in this book to represent total completeness of an item, can only indicate that these heads signify some type of universal dominion. Since Revelation 13:3-7 informs us that the Beast will eventually have world control, the 7 heads must represent a dominion over all of the geographical regions of the globe!

The Beast of Revelation 13 and the 11th horn of Daniel 7:20

A-10

And . . . interestingly enough, the *Readers Digest Atlas* (1963) tells us that there are SEVEN continental land masses on our globe: North America, South America, Europe, Asia, Africa, Australia, and Antarctica! **Thus this final world empire to be controlled by the Antichrist will not only be the Revived Roman Empire, but the evil system which emanates from this empire will in some way achieve world domination.** Just as the leaders of the Soviet Union today dominate much of the world outside of Russia, so in the last days the European Confederacy will through some diabolical system eventually rule the world!

An Empire of Anti-god Speech

That the word *"Blasphemy"* (anti-god speech) appears on each head of the Beast shows that this will be a world system based on wicked principles. Its leader, the 11th horn, the Antichrist, shall blaspheme, curse God, and persecute those who would turn to Christ during the entire awful final 3½ years of the Tribulation Period (Daniel 7:20, 21, 25). In fact, Revelation 13:4 clearly tells us that Satan himself is the unseen power behind this Beast system. This is why the Beast is identical in appearance to Satan, the Dragon (Revelation 12:3; 13:1)! Compare in contrast John 14:9.

The Clay of Daniel 2

In Daniel 2:40-44 the fourth and final world empire, the Roman Empire is shown as the iron legs of Nebuchadnezzar's dream image. Since it comes immediately after the ancient Greek Empire, which it replaces, and lasts until Christ's Second

Youth with Viet Cong flag atop statue in Washington, D.C. during Vietnam War. Terrorists activities which have burned across Europe and the Middle East will also engulf the United States. Insecure young people who have watched the erosion of supportive values and institutions, including family life, will usher in the age of lawlessness!

Coming, we know that this is the Roman Empire which will in some form survive unto the end of the age. If in the image vision the top of the iron legs are unified by having a garment covering the upper thighs then the history of the Roman Empire was to be as follows:

Empires Revealed

First, the unified upper legs denote a unified Rome which displaced the Greeks as the world power by the 2nd century B.C.; **Second,** the two iron legs show the division of the empire into two states, the Eastern and Western Roman Empires, by Diocletian in 300 A.D.; **Third,** the cracked feet signify in later days the empire's cracked and broken condition as the separate nations of Europe; **Fourth,** the ten toes are declared to be 10 kings (Daniel 2:41, 42, 44), and since Christ strikes these at His Coming we know that these are the 10 kings of the last days who give their allegiance over to the Antichrist (Revelation 17:12-13); and **Fifth,** a "miry clay" separates the strong Roman iron in the feet.

International Lawlessness

THIS CLAY (DANIEL 2:41-43) IS DESCRIBED AS SOME DIVISIVE FORCE OR PRINCIPLE OR SYSTEM WHICH SHALL PERVADE THE REVIVED EMPIRE IN ITS LAST DAYS—for it is mingled with the iron in the FEET which Christ smashes at His appearance at Armageddon. Immediately after this Christ sets up His Kingdom; Daniel 2:34ff).

Since this final clay-system is divisive, it tends to perpetuate divisions. What causes and perpetuates divisions among nations? Answer. Sin—treaty breaking, lying, undermining governments, false propaganda, attempting to gain unfair advantage, starting wars, causing revolutions, persecuting, etc. All of this in the world scene is a form of international LAWLESSNESS. Communism is the system that by both policy and practice perfectly fits this evil description!

The Beginning of Terrorism

In 2 Thessalonians 2:3 the Antichrist is called, *"the man of sin"*—which in the Greek literally translated would be, *ho avthropos fes anomias,* **"the man of LAWLESSNESS."** Thus Antichrist and the Beast Empire will be characterized by lawlessness, as well as by blasphemy and persecution (2 Thessalonians 2:3, 4; Revelation 13:1; Daniel 7:20-25). It will be Satan's empire and its persecution and blasphemy will be directed against Christ and His people (Revelation 13:4). Thus it is a *"scarlet Beast"* because it is red with the blood of the saints (Revelation 17:3).

Again, COMMUNISM is the system which fits. It is by its own admission anti-God, anti-Christ, anti-law, revolutionary and divisive. This Satanic system sprung into life in 1917 with Lenin and already it has devoured a billion people, a full one-third of the world! It has persecuted the saints already to a degree unparalleled in history sending more martyrs to their deaths in this century alone than have been slain in all the previous 19 centuries since Christ. It is growing wildly today across the world.

Thus the Beast in its final form will be some sort of European Confederacy of 10 nations, a Revived Roman Empire. **Its head is the Antichrist,** the 11th horn, whose personality and mind will become synonomous with that of the empire which he rules. This man and empire will grow until it has at least some degree of control over every region of the world. It will ferociously persecute those who will confess Christ and during the final 3½ years of the Tribulation it will kill them amid the greatest persecution the world has ever seen.

Today there is a system which fits this Beast, it is atheistic, materialistic, diabolical, anti-Christ, world COMMUNISM with its divisive spirit of revolution and its terrifying record of murder. We yet await the center of power to shift somehow from Moscow to a European Confederation, and then finally to "the man of lawlessness"—the Antichrist who is to arise.

Truly I think the above to be quite accurate—though the name of the system and even its emphasis may in the coming years be somewhat changed. We shall see—God knows. We, however, rather look forward to the Coming of Christ at the Rapture (1 Thessalonians 4:13-18), and we remember our Saviour's words of Luke 21:28.

> And when these things begin to come to pass, then look up, and lift up your heads; for your redemption draweth nigh.

An artist's conception of how the Rapture may occur. Some in your family may be left behind!

Their critics call them fanatics. But these Jews maintain that Israel has no right to exist until the coming of the Messiah.

This religious group believes that the Jews were sent by God into exile in punishment for sin, and until the Messiah comes, they, the Jews, should take no forcible action to regain the Holy Land.

In Yasser Arafat, leader of the PLO, they see a natural ally in their opposition to the present Jewish state.

In fact, it has been reported that if a Palestine government-in-exile would be formed, some of these anti-Zionist Jews would be included in it.

Steps to Subservience

How does the pattern of world domination change so that new governments rise to control?

We can see that pattern developing even today.

In the opinion of this author, the United States, once looked upon as the major power of the world, will soon sink into a second-rate power. The soaring debt of the United States is rapidly getting out of hand. The **debt** of the American people, of business and of government combined in 1978 was over 3 trillion dollars! **This is nearly two thirds more than just five years ago!**

Public debt in 1978 reached the 750-billion mark.

Yet during the 1974-75 recession Americans took the attitude of "eat, drink and be merry," realizing that tomorrow offered little hope. They bought luxury-priced cars and went on a travel binge to resorts worldwide, trying to forget their problems.

Sports has become an obsession with many Americans ... so much so that TV broadcasters paid $60 million last year just for the opportunity to televise football games. Now roughly 1000 hours of TV time a year are devoted to big-time sports. This is double the number in 1970.

Reliving the Days of Rome

In ancient Rome, they imposed heavy taxes in order to support sports activities. In the United States, since 1960, an estimated $1 billion worth of municipally supported arenas have been built and paid for by taxpayers. Now, with stadiums only half-filled, taxpayers will have to shell out close to $1 billion more to cover deficits.

In New Orleans, Louisiana, citizens built an enclosed Superdome. The dome itself, which was to cost $35 million and be self-supporting, now is costing some $163 million plus tens of millions in interest costs!

Contracts for players have soared to as high as $2 million for multi-year arrangements!

Meanwhile an estimated 34 million dogs in the United States require a pet-control program of some $500 million, much of it going for destroying unwanted animals.

More than $300 million was spent by Americans in 1978 to buy pets. And more than $2 billion is spent a year on pet food.

**Dog Food
Surpasses
Baby Food**

The largest-selling dry or canned food item in grocery stores is pet food; four times more than baby food sales!

Besides this Americans spend about $2 billion a year on dog accessories — including gem-studded collars, perfume, gold-plated license tags, beef-flavored toothpaste and breath sprays. Dogs have their own motels, with wall-to-wall carpeting, brass beds and piped-in music.

There are stores which will outfit your dog in designer clothes. And grooming salons exist which will give your dog an egg shampoo.

Now, granted, only a few dogs enjoy such luxuries . . . but this is an indication of the misplaced emphasis on life that is rotting American leadership and strength and dissipating its financial stability in the eyes of the world.

Our soaring national debt, our obsession with material possessions and luxuries, our growing crime rate are but a few indicators that make it evident that soon, perhaps in the next 25 years, we will find it necessary to merge with other nations for our very existence. We are already moving in this direction and have taken the first step to subservience . . . a step that one day will lead to the emergence of a powerful World Leader!

**A World
Goes Hungry**

While we bask in comparative luxury, most of the world is struggling for its very life. The starving 75 million people of

Nations
Will
Starve

Bangladesh will be, according to projections, a starving 150 million people in just 25 years. The 800 million hungry people of the Indian subcontinent will balloon to 1.6 billion hungry people.

There is popular thinking today that perhaps the best approach to resolving world problems is to let people in poor nations simply starve to death. One scientist wrote in the October, 1974 issue of **BioScience:**

> Every life saved this year in a poor country diminishes the quality of life for subsequent generations.
>
> Every rich nation amounts to a lifeboat full of comparatively rich people. The poor of the world are in other, much more crowded lifeboats.
>
> Continuously, so to speak, the poor fall out of their lifeboats and swim for a little while in the water outside, hoping to be admitted to a rich lifeboat . . . What should the passengers on the rich lifeboat do?
>
> It's true we can support a great many more people than we are supporting today. If the United States turns completely vegetarian, our agriculture can support 800 million people instead of 200 million.
>
> But the world is increasing at 90 million people a year, so that only gives us nine years. What do you do for an encore after those nine years?

And that becomes the problem? What will happen in 1985? Will all the hopes of all the years be suddenly dampened by disaster? I believe it will. Perhaps, not exactly in 1985 . . . but by 1990!

A
Dire
Prediction

The Club of Rome, a group of scientists and professors, seem to agree that time, indeed is running out! The very aspects of population growth are overwhelming. By the end of the next century, the world economy could be over 50 times its present size! By the year 2000, Southeast Asia will have a 30% food deficit — which will be 100% in the year 2025!

By the year 2025 world population growth **each year** will be equivalent to the **total** of the first 1,500 years A.D.!

Right now some 400 to 500 million children suffer from malnutrition worldwide. In 1965 emergency food reserves amounted to 80 days of consumption. Today, they have been reduced to under 30 days of consumption!

The
Potential
for
Destruction

Today it takes 7-8 years to construct one relatively simple nuclear reactor to provide us with power. In 100 years, with population growth quadrupled what it is today, to satisfy energy demands, we will need 3000 "nuclear parks."

Now here are the dire consequences! Plutonium, a radioactive element, capable of self-maintained explosive fission, is used as fuel in nuclear reactors.

With proper precautions it does not present a danger. But it will become necessary, for mere human existence, to construct many more "nuclear parks" than we have today.

Scientists say it is like making a contract

A
Contract
With The
Devil

with the Devil in order to buy a little more time and to exist. Just ten one-millionths of a gram of Plutonium is enough to produce lung cancer. And a Plutonium ball the size of a grapefruit contains enough poison to annihilate the population of this planet!

Furthermore, plutonium's radioactivity lasts 25,000 years!

Clearly we have come to the end of the Golden Age.

The Center for Defense Information, a private U.S. organization states that the United States has an arsenal of over 35,000 nuclear weapons, 15,800 which are stored in the U.S. and the rest scattered throughout the world. It further stated the U.S. is producing nuclear weapons at the rate of three per day.

Rear Admiral Gene R. La Rocque said:

> These weapons carry a combined explosive capability equivalent to an estimated 460 million tons of TNT — roughly 35,000 times greater than the nuclear weapon that destroyed Hiroshima in 1945.

Over 70,000 died at Hiroshima!

The
Changing of
Power

What does all this have to do with Israel?

Someone once said, "Nothing in the world occurs which does not, either directly or indirectly, affect everyone else."

How can the fact that the United States must dole out food stamps to some 20 million Americans affect Israel? It is but another step that one day will lead, in the author's opinion, to so taxing America's viability that it will cause America to join a European bloc of nations that will give birth to Antichrist . . . dreaded enemy of the Jew.

More Dependency On Government

The very fact that more and more Americans are relying on government for their food and for their life . . . places people in a mood of subservience to a leader. The way is being prepared for tomorrow's mold of dictatorship!

And the dilemma is that in early 1975 the U.S. signed a contract worth $77 million dollars with a private American firm to teach Saudi Arabian troops how to protect the world's richest oil fields. Under this contract 1000 former U.S. servicemen were to be sent to Saudi Arabia to train four battalions of the 26,000-man National Guard there.

In one year alone the U.S. sold over $4 billion worth of weapons to Iran, Saudi Arabia, Kuwait and Oman. This was about half the total of all foreign arms sales that year!

Also helping the Arab cause are the British, the French and the Soviet Union. The Soviet Union is selling tanks, fighter and attack planes, bombers and missiles to Syria and Iraq at a $2-billion-a-year pace.

In 1975 Spain bought more than $200 million worth of U.S. fighter planes. Iran purchased six fast destroyers from the U.S.

The international trade in non-nuclear arms now tops $20 billion annually — a jump of more than 550% since 1964!

The paradox of war! While Israeli soldiers unload artillery shells at a border post, the U.S. is training Saudi Arabian pilots in Texas and supplying millions of dollars of arms to both sides.

**United States
Largest
Arms Merchant**

And the nations of the world, in 1974 spent over $250 billion to train, equip and maintain their armed forces!

The United States (who sells freely to both Arab and Jew — and wonders why everyone doesn't love us) is easily the world's largest arms merchant . . . selling over $100 billion since 1950. The Soviet Union is the second largest. The U.S. shipped 600 tanks alone to Israel in 1975; and even its own army was short 1500 tanks!

Since the 1973 war, Israel has obtained more than $2 billion in supersonic fighter-bombers, tanks, bombs and ammunition.

One successful European arms trader commenting on his rising wealth said quite honestly:

We still deal in original sin.

What does this all spell? The exploding population, the rising U.S. debt, the scramble for arms superiority? Quite frankly, it spells crisis . . . catastrophe . . . and a change in the power domination of the world.

This changing of power, I believe, may occur within the next 15 years. Assassinations and coups have a way of changing power structures overnight.

14

THE FORCES OF ANTICHRIST EMERGING

**The Rise
of
European
Supremacy**

The enlarged European community has replaced the United States as the leading world trading power. Together, these European nations now have a Gross National Product that is over three-fourths that of the United States. They control three and a half times the currency reserves of the United States. In 1950, the United States held 50% of the world's monetary reserves. It now holds only 8%. But the Europe of the Nine (Common Market nations) now hold over 40%!

It has been said that great nations go through a 200-year cycle:

From bondage to freedom
From freedom back to bondage

Will this be the path the United States will take? Only time will tell.

West Germany, an economic giant, is now assuming a greater role of leadership in this time of world economic crisis. In 1974 West Germany had a $22 billion trade surplus and nearly $40 billion in gold. It was Henry Kissinger who requested that West Germany play a more active role in the Arab oil crisis, supporting the U.S. But the Europeans insist on having their own policy in the Middle East . . . a policy they can control!

**The Day
Millions
Suddenly
Disappear**

There will come a day . . . no one knows when . . . when millions of believers will suddenly disappear from this earth! This may be hard for many readers to accept and believe.

But if they study God's Word, the Bible, they will discover that there are more than 300 Old and New Testament Scriptures which promise that Jesus Christ will come again!

And these promises will be fulfilled just as literally as the 200 Old Testament prophecies of His virgin birth, death, burial and resurrection were fulfilled in His first coming when He suffered and died for man's sin.

This event, when millions of believers disappear, is called the Rapture. It is the first phase of the events of the Second Coming of Christ.[1]

---

[1]The Rapture refers to the time, prior to the start of the 7 year Tribulation Period, when believing Christians (both dead and alive) will "in the twinkling of an eye" be *caught up (raptured)* to meet Christ in the air. See 1 Thessalonians 4:14-17. For a comprehensive view of this event, we suggest you read GUIDE TO SURVIVAL by Salem Kirban, pp. 124-143.

When this event occurs, the mood and character of nations may change dramatically. The alignment of nations may also change. The patterns of nation alignment and power we are witnessing today will reach their final fulfillment in the 7-year Tribulation Period which follows the Rapture.

The Reviving of the Roman Empire

The last of the seven Gentile world powers to persecute the nation of Israel will be the Revived Roman Empire.

What were the seven Gentile world powers? Revelation 12:3; 13:1; and 17:7 refer to these powers as seven heads. They seem to be:

1. **Egypt**
   Egypt enslaved Israel for 400 years.
   See Exodus 1-12.

2. **Assyria**
   Assyria captured and scattered the Northern Kingdom of Israel.
   See 2 Kings 17.

3. **Babylon**
   Babylon captured and took away the Southern Kingdom of Israel.
   See 2 Kings 24.

4. **Medes & Persians**
   These nations produced wicked Haman and Darius.
   See Esther 3, Isaiah 13.

5. **Greece**
   Greece brought Alexander the Great and later produced Antiochus Epiphanes, the persecutor.

See Daniel 8 and 11.

6. Rome

Rome destroyed Jerusalem in 70 AD.
See Luke 21.

7. Revived Roman Empire

The Revived Roman Empire will become Israel's greatest persecutor!
See Revelation 12.

The old Roman Empire was quite extensive both geographically and politically. It included England, most of Europe, Asia Minor, Syria, Palestine, Egypt and the northern part of Africa.

What countries will comprise the Revived Roman Empire from which Antichrist will emerge? No one knows for certain. It would seem to cover territorially today's 9 Common Market nations which includes England. We do know, according to God's Word, that 10 nations will comprise the final bloc from which Antichrist will become leader.

I believe it is possible that the United States will become that tenth nation . . . going back to her mother, England, and merging with the 9 nations for her very economic existence.

There will be some who will disagree with this, of course. Only time will reveal exactly what nations will make up this revived Roman Empire structure.

**Energy Crisis
A Prelude**

The United States torn between whether it should support the Arab nations or Israel . . . sided finally with Israel. Promptly the

Arab nations stopped the flow of oil to the United States.

This sparked the famous November 7, 1973 Energy Crisis speech by President Richard Nixon. Gas stations were ordered closed on Sundays, a 55-mile per hour speed limit was enforced nationally.

"Spy on your Neighbor" programs began to rear their ugly head as some states suggested phoning a Complaint Center for those who waste energy.

Christmas tree lights were dimmed. Churches cancelled Christmas Eve services. The nation and the world suddenly were caught in the mass hysteria of world trials . . . while a courier of peace, Henry Kissinger, flew furiously back and forth to China, to Russia and to Brussels and Geneva striving to restore peace.

These events are a prelude and a prototype of the chaos that will occur during the initial reign of Antichrist.

Time will certainly reveal the answers to these questions.

Aligning
Our
Priorities

The important thing for the reader to know is not necessarily who Antichrist is but to recognize his need for the Saviour and to accept Jesus Christ as his personal Saviour and Lord.

If however, this is not done — you will recognize the Antichrist by the description we have given as to what he will do when he does come.

God alone can give genuine peace. Jesus is

known as the Prince of Peace. Antichrist will try to take over this role and produce a so-called heaven on earth.

We will see the world become very enthusiastic about his reign and indeed some very marvelous things will be produced at that time. Great new cities may be built and science will no doubt make startling discoveries.

This will be an era in which man will be exalted to the skies but in Obadiah 1:4 the Lord promises:

> Though thou exalt thyself as the eagle, and though thou set thy nest among the stars, thence will I bring thee down, saith the Lord.

If you live during the reign of Antichrist . . . don't be fooled by his message of peace . . . for his main purpose is to bring a reign of death and destruction!

The Beginning of the Numbering System

A news article, published in TIME, March 13, 1972, commenting on a critical Senate Finance Committee vote on the issuing of a Social Security number at age 6, reported:

> "Such a system would further enable the Government to amass information on citizens and store it in a central computer under a single identification number. To date, no one has suggested using tattoos."

On March 3, 1972 the Senate Finance Committee voted to direct the U.S. Government to issue a Social Security card to every child entering the first grade after January 1, 1974. Its purpose is to make the Social Security number the universal form

Very shortly all supermarkets will have computer check-out stations to automatically add up your purchases through product identification codes on each item. This same computer will approve or deny you the power to buy and deduct the purchase from your bank account.

of identification for everyone in the U.S.

Such a system will enable the Government to begin to amass information on each individual at a very early age.

We have become acclimated to numbering systems. The first one to make a widespread use of a number was Adolf Hitler during World War 2. During that war he had the Jews tattooed with identification numbers on their forearms after they were placed in concentration camps.

Pick up the phone to make a telephone call. You dial an area code number. Mail a letter. You use a zip code number. Make a purchase in Sears or any large department store and your credit card with a number is punched into a special new computer that relays that number to a clearing house. Within a few split seconds the machine indicates whether your purchase is approved or denied.

Open a checking account . . . and your checks will bear a magnetic code number. Subscribe to a magazine . . . and you receive a computer number on a card which states, "Do not fold, spindle or mutilate."

Computer Buying in the Supermarkets

In certain locations in Ohio, experiments have been conducted on making purchases in the local supermarket by a special magnetic card. After making purchases, the card is inserted into the computer. The clerk dials a number which connects his keyboard with the local bank. Within 15 seconds your purchases are either ac-

YOUR NAME IS SURE TO BE IN ONE OF THESE COMPUTERS

The United States government knows you by a number. And federal agencies are turning to computers . . . which, at the touch of a button . . . can produce instant information on millions of Americans. Here are some major examples:

SOCIAL SECURITY ADMINISTRATION
Your Social Security number will soon become a universal number.

INTERNAL REVENUE SERVICE
Computer tapes store details from tax returns of over 75 million citizens. These tapes are made available to the 50 States.

U.S. SECRET SERVICE
About 50,000 persons are on computer who might tend to harm or embarrass the President or other high Government officials.

F.B.I.
Fingerprint files of over 86 million people now on computer.

DEPARTMENT OF AGRICULTURE
Keeps data on over 850,000 people.

DEPARTMENT OF TRANSPORTATION
Almost 2.7 million citizens who have been denied driver's licenses are on computer.

PENTAGON
Maintains files on some 7 million military personnel and civilians who have been subjected to "security, loyalty, criminal and other type investigations."

VETERANS ADMINISTRATION
Keeps files on 13.5 million veterans and dependents.

DEPARTMENT OF LABOR
Has on computer files on 2 million persons in federally financed work . . . all coded by their social security number.

DEPARTMENT OF JUSTICE
Computer bank has names of more than 14,000 individuals who have been involved in riots and civil disorders since mid-1968.

DEPARTMENT of HOUSING and URBAN DEVELOPMENT
Maintains records on 4.5 million who have bought F.H.A. homes.

With this federal computer network, there is virtually no limit to the volume of information that can be made available at a moment's notice on just about every American.

cepted . . . or if your account is in arrears, you place the food back on the shelves!

Federal Government computers maintain millions of files covering every individual in the United States . . . and these are instantly available at the flick of a switch.

West Germany has already issued a 12-digit number to everyone in that country—this number will accompany its holder from cradle to grave.

By 1984, most transactions will be made by a card identification system. Cash will become unpopular. It is quite possible that an invisible tattoo number system for identification will be introduced which becomes visible under special lights.

15

WHO IS ANTICHRIST?

The World's Most Popular Individual

There have been many views expounded on exactly who Antichrist will be.

However, it is important to keep in mind that Antichrist will **not** be revealed until after the Rapture (When the saints rise to meet Christ in the air).

After the Christians are taken up from earth to meet Christ at the Rapture — then the person of Antichrist will be identified and revealed. According to 2 Thessalonians 2:4, the proof of his identity comes when he sits in the rebuilt Temple in Jerusalem and declares himself to be God.

The Bible does give us some key characteristics that will expose his true identity as Antichrist.

1. **He will be popular and worshipped!**
   ...the whole earth was amazed and followed after the beast [Antichrist] ... and they worshiped the beast ... (Revelation 13:3, 4).

2. **He will be fearless!**
   ... Who is the beast [Antichrist], and

who is able to wage war with him? (Revelation 13:4)

3. **He will persecute the Tribulation Saints!**
   And it was given to him to make war with the saints and to overcome them . . . (Revelation 13:7)

4. **He will be a world dictator!**
   . . . authority over every tribe and people and tongue and nation was given to him (Revelation 13:7).

5. **He will be a maker of peace treaties!**
   And he will make a firm covenant [treaty] with many for one week [one "seven year period"] with Israel (Daniel 9:27).

6. **He will not honor his peace treaty!**
   . . . in the middle of the week [at 3½ years] he will put a stop to sacrifice . . . and on the wing of abominations will come one who makes desolate, even until a complete destruction . . . is poured out on the one who makes desolate (Daniel 9:27).

   He will break his pledge and stop the Jews from all their sacrifices, and as a climax to his terrible deeds, he will defile the sanctuary of God.

7. **He will have no respect for the religion of his race; nor will he embrace any religious conviction!**
   And he will show no regard for the gods of his fathers . . . nor will he show regard for any other god; for he will magnify himself above them all (Daniel 11:37).

8. **He will change territorial boundaries!**
   . . . he will give great honor to those who acknowledge him, and he will cause them to rule over many, and shall divide the land for gain (Daniel 11:39).

9. **He will be a skilled negotiator!**
   And at the latter end of their kingdom, when the transgressors [the apostate Jews]

Sydney J. Harris

Wanted--a False Messiah

Reprinted by request.

People keep saying "We need a leader" or "We need better leadership," but that is not what they really mean. What most of them are looking for is not a leader, but a Messiah.

They want someone who will give them the Word. And the Word would be one that is agreeable to them, that appeals to their preferences and prejudices, so they can follow it wholeheartedly.

the common good and for the good of their own souls. He is never followed by very many, usually killed by the majority, and venerated only when he is safely dead and need not be taken seriously.

What we are looking for, I am afraid, is neither a true leader nor a true Messiah, but a false Messiah — a man who will give us over-simplified answers, who will justify our ways, who will castigate our enemies, who will vindicate our selfishness as a way of life, and make us comfortable within our ~~prejudices and preconceptions~~.

'Chromosome Passports' For All Forecast by Experts

JERUSALEM, Sept. 16 (Agence France-Presse)—Scientist here forecast this week that before long every person would carry a "chromosome passport" issued at birth by a computerized machine.

Professionally called a karyotype, the passport would contain the genetic analysis of the individual and would be carried like blood-group tags by soldiers and many civilians, the scientists said. Couples contemplating marriage will be expected to exchange karyotypes as well as general health certificates.

This was forecast at the fourth international chromosome conference in Jerusalem, attended by 150 participants from 22 countries.

*have reached the fullness [of their wicked-
ness, exceeding the limits of God's mercy],
a king of fierce countenance and understanding dark trickery and craftiness, shall
stand up (Daniel 8:23).*

10. **His armies will be destroyed and he will be
cast alive into the Lake of Fire!**
    *And the beast [Antichrist] was seized, and
    with him the false prophet who performed
    the signs in his presence, by which he de-
    ceived those who had received the mark of
    the beast [666] and those who worshiped
    his image; these two were thrown alive into
    the lake of fire which burns with brimstone.
    And the rest were killed with the sword . . .
    (Revelation 19:20, 21).*

**Antichrist
Could Be
Living Today!**

There is some indication in Scripture that
the Antichrist may be active on the world
scene even before the Tribulation Period
begins. This is based on 2 Thessalonians
2:3:

*Don't be carried away and deceived re-
gardless of what they say. For that day will
not come until two things happen: first,
there will be a time of great rebellion
against God, and then the man of rebellion
will come—the son of hell (The Living New
Testament).*

Then in verse 8 of the same chapter we
read:

*Then this wicked one will appear, whom
the Lord Jesus will burn up with the breath
of His mouth and destroy by His presence
when He returns.*

From this it would appear that the Antichrist may be known to us (but not identi-
fiable as Antichrist) before the Rapture occurs.

However, this is important. His real, diabolical, Satanic *character* is revealed only at the middle of the Tribulation, when he demands a type of worship which can only rightly be given unto God.

It is not God's purpose to reveal everything to us in this day and age.

Will Iraq's Babylon Rise Again?

(Some Bible scholars have even suggested that Antichrist, taking advantage of the unsettled conditions in the Middle East, will establish himself as the ruler of Iraq, the land upon which the ancient city of Babylon once stood.

In time they think he will attack and subdue three member states of the Mediterranean Confederacy which from then on will be ruled by Iraq as the center of this newly acquired empire.

This would make the prophetic "Babylon" of Revelation 17 and 18 literally Babylon Rebuilt. You will recall that Babylon was the center of the nations' first rebellion against God as recorded in the Tower of Babel episode in Genesis.)

What about his religion? Religiously, he will deny all authority but his own authority. He is called in Scriptures—The Lawless One.

The October, 1973 "Yom Kippur" War in the Middle East brought new problems to the world unleashing an avalanche of events that are drawing us even closer to the time of the Rapture.

The fourth Arab-Israeli war since the

foundation of the Jewish state in 1948 spawned a host of perils. Not only did the combatants pay a fearsome price in blood and treasure but the conflict drew the United States and Russia into a near confrontation.

16

REVEALING THE SATANIC TRINITY

**A Friend
to Both
Jew and Gentile**

One of these days some great leader, admired by the world as a man of peace will offer to settle the Arab-Israeli dispute.

Watch out when this event happens. For this man will be what the Scriptures term **Antichrist.**

And his sweet words of peace will soon lead to the most devastating seven years of terror, trials, and wholesale murders. This 7-year time period will occur after the **Rapture**[1]. It will be known as the **Tribulation Period**[2].

The **Antichrist** is a part of the Satanic Trinity just as **Christ** is part of the Heavenly Trinity.

It is important that we know the definition before we get further into the subject.

**The
Satanic
Trinity**

Just as the Heavenly Trinity is made up of the:

1. Father
2. Son
3. Holy Spirit,

so likewise in the counterfeit Trinity the members are:

1. **Satan**
   He is sometimes referred in the Scriptures as the Dragon and is known as anti-God. He imitates the work of God the Father (Revelation 12:9; 20:2).

2. **Antichrist**
   He is sometimes referred in the Scriptures as the Beast. Antichrist imitates the work of God the Son (Revelation 13:1; 19:20).

3. **The False Prophet**
   He is sometimes referred in the Scriptures as the Second Beast. The False Prophet imitates the work of God the Holy Spirit (Revelation 13:11; 19:20).

The word **Antichrist** means an enemy of Christ or one who usurps Christ's name and authority.

1
RAPTURE
This refers to the time, prior to the start of the 7-year Tribulation Period, when believing Christians (both dead and alive) will *"in the twinkling of an eye"* rise up to meet Christ in the air. Read 1 Thessalonians 4:13-17 in the New Testament.

2
TRIBULATION PERIOD
This will be a period of 7 years, following the Rapture, of phenomenal world trial and suffering. It is at this time that Antichrist will reign over a federation of 10 nations which quite possibly could include the Common Market nations and the United States. See Daniel 9:27 and Matthew 24:21.

Because Antichrist will temporarily be able to resolve the problems of the Middle East, Arabs and Jews alike will welcome him as the Peacemaker!

As you may recall, 2 Thessalonians 2:1-12 refers to the Antichrist as "that man of sin" and states that he will oppose and exalt himself above God and will actually sit in the temple of God and claim to be God.

Antichrist and the False Prophet

Both the Antichrist and the False Prophet will be living during what is termed as the Tribulation Period.

This Tribulation Period will last for seven years. The second 3½ years especially will be filled with terror, death and destruction.

The False Prophet, however, does not try to promote himself and should not be confused with the Antichrist.

The False Prophet never becomes an object of worship. He does the work of a prophet by directing attention away from himself and towards the Antichrist whom he says has the right to be worshipped (Revelation 13:12).

Both the Antichrist and the False Prophet are tools in the hands of Satan and their every move will be guided by Satan.

It is quite interesting to note that Jesus Christ in John 5:43 seems to have made a prophetic reference to the Antichrist when He said:

"I am come in my Father's name, and ye receive me not: if another shall come in his own name, him ye will receive."

Antichrist to be Welcomed by the Jews

It is also sad to reflect that the Jews rejected Jesus Christ as their Messiah—but when the Antichrist comes they will be deceived by him and accept him and welcome him with open arms as their king and saviour.

In Daniel 11:36, 37 we are told that the Antichrist will ". . . exalt himself, and magnify himself above every god. . . ."

And in 2 Thessalonians 2:4 it is revealed, ". . . so that he as God sitteth in the temple of God, shewing himself that he is God."

There are indications in the Bible that Antichrist will become popular because of the prevailing lawlessness that occurs throughout the world and his **supposed ability** to resolve world problems.

Satan the Great Imitator

Since Satan is the great imitator of God . . . during the first half of the Tribulation Period, or before, Satan permits Israel to rebuild the temple that he might at this place and in this temple erected to God, transfer worship from God to himself.

And where Jehovah had put His name . . . Satan in turn sets up his image and working through the False Prophet, who directs worship to the Antichrist, leads the Jews astray and fulfills that part of prophecy which was quoted before as saying:

> I am come in my Father's name, and ye receive me not; if another shall come in his own name, him ye will receive (John 5:43).

So here we find many Jews welcoming and worshipping Antichrist thinking that he is from God.

The sad fact is that the prophets of the Old Testament had prophesied of this day and Jesus, too, had warned Israel, more than 1900 years ago, about this coming tribulation period.

Jeremiah spoke of this in the Old Testament, referring to it as the time of Jacob's trouble, when he said in Jeremiah 30:7:

Alas! for that day is great, so that none is like it; it is even the time of Jacob's trouble, but he shall be saved out of it.

And we are fast approaching the day which Jeremiah, Isaiah, Daniel and the Lord Jesus and others had prophesied.

Satan will Fulfill Prophecy

Now Satan will be fulfilling these prophecies exactly as they had been written. Antichrist will assume power and the temple will be erected. **And because Israel refuses to worship Satan as God, there will follow one of the greatest slaughters in history as Jacob's trouble begins.**

This shows the power of sin! God has given both the Jews and the Gentiles signs in the heaven and earth, but these are mocked by the people of this day. Is it no wonder that the Bible tells us:

But as the days of Noah were, so shall also the coming of the Son of man be (Matthew 24:37).

The tragedy is that even under these new judgments which redouble with intensity, the world will still continue to worship Satan and not believe in the true God.

This will be the condition of the world at the close of the first 3½ years of the Tribu-

In the middle of the Tribulation Period the world leader who has befriended the people of Israel will suddenly begin his transition to terror. His first step will be to desecrate the Temple in Israel . . . possibly removing the Altar and placing his statue in the identical area.

lation Period.

What is now left for God to do when He is rejected of men?

The only thing left for Him to do is to follow His plan for the development of His kingdom during this closing period when there are false teachers and false preachers and people believing and worshipping a lie.

Therefore, He allows the second 3½ years of the Tribulation Period to occur in which this trial by fire awakens many thousands to accepting Christ as their personal Saviour and brings the Jew back to the fold into acknowledging Christ as Messiah, Saviour, Redeemer and Lord.

This is one of the reasons why the second half of the Tribulation Period, commonly known as "Jacob's trouble," must come to pass.

Satan's Role in the Tribulation Period

During the first 3½ years Antichrist (the world ruler) and the False Prophet (the world church leader) have so fooled the world into believing that they are truly called of God and have truly brought peace to the earth . . . that now Satan can move into the next phase of his program and cause the people of the world to bow down and worship him.

To those who refuse, their refusal will heap on their heads terror and tragedy.

Jerusalem, the city of Peace, has been the scene of many bloody conflicts.

But God promised that the time would

come when that city would be rebuilt and extended according to His blueprint. He also promised that after this the city would not be destroyed again.

We find this in Jeremiah 31:38-40:

> Behold, the days come, saith the Lord, that the city shall be built to the Lord from the tower of Hananeel unto the gate of the corner. (38)

> And the measuring line shall yet go forth over against it upon the hill Gareb, and shall compass about to Goath. (39)

> And the whole valley of the dead bodies, and of the ashes, and all the fields unto the brook of Kidron, unto the corner of the horse gate toward the east, shall be holy unto the Lord; it shall not be plucked up, nor thrown down any more for ever. (40)

Antichrist will use all deceptive means at his disposal to command the people of the world . . . even to promising peace!

17

THE PEACEMAKER WHO BECOMES
PERSECUTOR

**The
Reign
of
Antichrist**

Antichrist will be an extremely popular individual. He will pose as a great humanitarian and the friend of men. **He will appear to be a very special friend to the Jewish race.** There is no doubt from the Scriptures that he will persuade the Jews that he has come to usher in the golden age for the Jewish race. In light of this they will receive him as their Messiah.

> One might say that he is a "composite man" who will have an irresistible personality. Because of his versatile accomplishments, super-human wisdom, and great administrative and executive ability he will be looked upon with favor by all of the world leaders and populace.

Along with his powers as a brilliant diplomat he will be a superb strategist in the art of war.

Keep in mind that this Antichrist will come into prominence during the Tribulation Period. At the moment of the Rapture, there will not be left one single believer on this earth.

So basically at the beginning of the Tribulation Period, everyone on the earth will be an unbeliever and look to this Antichrist with great fascination and believe that he offers the world life-saving salvation.

One thing is certain from the many references found regarding the Antichrist in the Scriptures: He will be a counterfeit and a clever imitation of the true Christ.

> *His rise will be sudden*
> *This also will be an imitation of Christ.*

You will recall that Christ for 30 years remained in obscurity in his home in Nazareth and the silence of those years is broken only once in Luke 2.

Comparatively, the Antichrist will also remain in obscurity and then suddenly his rise will be brought into prominence. He may even now be in the world and preparing for his Satan-directed work.

He Promises Peace

As was stated before, undoubtedly one of the elements of his marvelous success in gaining the hearts of the people lies in the fact that he will come promising the very thing that is uppermost in the hearts of people all over the world today: PEACE!

This man, in the person of Antichrist, will accomplish this very thing . . . but what most people do not realize is that this accomplishment will be only for a little season—and then the very gates of hell will break loose here on earth.

His First Move

One of the first moves of the Antichrist will be to gain the confidence of the Jewish people and others by his diplomatically settling the then explosive Middle East situation.

Therefore, his first attempt is to gain the favor of the Jewish people.

After accomplishing this, he will help the Jewish people immeasurably probably by returning many of them to the land of Israel and he will show them many favors.

Actually the Tribulation Period will begin with a public appearance of Antichrist when he participates in the making of a significant seven year Middle East peace pact (Daniel 9:27). At this time, however, he will not yet be recognized as the Antichrist. This recognition awaits another 3½ years (Matthew 24:15).

His Master Plan

This individual will eventually be the head of what may be known as the Federated States of Europe. As the head of this organization, he would be able to exert great authority and power by attempting to settle the Arab-Israeli dispute.

The Scriptures seem to indicate that he will side with Israel in backing her claim to the land of Palestine.

Russia will be a part of a northern confederacy and will back the Arab's claim to Palestine.

The following verses in 2 Thessalonians 2 and Ezekiel 38 exhibit this prophecy.

> And thou (Russia) shalt come from thy place out of the north parts . . . all of them riding upon horses . . . a mighty army: And thou shalt come up against my people of Israel . . . surely in that day there shall be a great shaking in the land of Israel (Ezekiel 38:15, 16, 19).

> And then shall that Wicked (Antichrist) be revealed, whom the Lord shall consume with the spirit of his mouth . . . whose coming is after the working of Satan with all power and signs and lying wonders (2 Thessalonians 2:8, 9).

It is estimated today that there are some 3 million Jews living in Israel.

To some extent they are reviving many of their distinctive historic features and customs. However, surveys show that the religious faith of the vast majority of Jews is neither Biblical Judaism nor Christianity.

Most of them hold to a liberalized Judaism religion and some of them, as in the case of so many of today's population, are even atheists.

There are very few Jews in Israel who accept Jesus Christ as the true Messiah or look to God literally to fulfill Old Testament prophecies.

In spite of this, however, they still look upon the land of Palestine as the country of great promise for them.

Why would Russia want to invade Palestine or Israel?

Scientists have discovered that all of the manufactured goods, fruits and vegetables exported from this land of Israel are nothing in comparison with the mineral wealth of the Dead Sea.

Since the days of Abraham which were four thousands of years ago, God has been pouring into this mysterious sea a fabulous amount of wealth in the form of mineral salts.

Only with the return of the Jews to this land, have attempts been made to discover the mineral content of the Dead Sea. The analysis shows that the value of the chemicals in the Dead Sea is $1,270,000,000,000. It is believed that this staggering sum is equal to the combined wealth of the United States, Great Britain, France, Germany and Italy.

Antichrist an Irresistible Personality

As we stated before, the Antichrist will continue to rise for 3½ years and then he will reign for 3½ years (Revelation 13:5). This is the length of the Tribulation Period. He will be President of the 10 Federated Nations. These nations may be known as the Federated States of Europe.

While it is true that at present the great problem facing the Western powers today is the problem of trying to bring together, under the same head, nations that were originally part of the same Roman Empire . . . this problem will be erased in the near future.

Common Market Headquarters in Brussels, Belgium. Antichrist, quite possibly could become the head of this union of nations. Turn this page and you will note this building is shaped in the form of a stylized cross.

The 10 Federated States of Europe will probably include France, England and Germany (possibly West Germany) as well as lesser countries, and perhaps the United States.

The prophecy is revealed in Revelation (17:12-13), which shows that these nations that were once a part of the Roman Empire will gather together and are going to enter into an agreement to give their authority to one man as their head (Daniel 7:7-8, 23-26 compared with Revelation 13).

This one man will be the Antichrist.

A man more subtle and more powerful than Hitler will arise!

18

THE MAN OF PEACE BECOMES
THE MAN OF WAR

To those in Israel, the first 3½ years will seem like a heaven on earth.

They are back in their land. The Antichrist has fulfilled his promises in bringing peace to the land and protecting the Jews from the onrushing armies of Russia and her allies.

His Rise Will be Sudden

Jerusalem is looked up to as one of the most elite cities of the world and is the hub of business activity, fashion and world culture.

It would appear that Utopia had arrived. At last the world could now settle down to a world of peace under the protectorate of a great world leader who has amassed under him the cooperation of the 10 powerful states known as the European Federation of States.

But the honeymoon soon will be over and the next 3½ years (the last half of the Tribulation Period) ushers in a most horrible period of death and destruction for both the Jews and those who then will turn to Christ.

The Treaty Broken

How does this all begin and why does it occur?

The ten-dictatorship confederation of nations will, for some reason, decide that one man should have rule over them. However, three of the ten nations will disagree. At this point, Antichrist, will be able to crush this rebellion, and in so doing, will emerge in strength (Daniel 7:20).

A similar pattern developed during the early Hitler days, where Hitler was able, through deceitful means, to quell his opposition. Through this success he was able to become the leader not only of Germany, but also of other European nations.

Israel's Darkest Day

Once established as the principal ruler of this 10-nation Federation, which may be called the United States of Europe, Antichrist will seek to wield his political diplomacy.

The Arab-Israeli conflict, long a sore point and threat to world peace, is, after Russia's demise in power, Antichrist's first major challenge.

Without doubt, Antichrist will present himself as a protector of Israel. In the beginning he perhaps will pledge himself to re-establish them en masse in Israel and restore to them any territory they may have ceded through treaties to the Arabs. This will probably also be a treaty of non-aggression and will be just as valid as the so-called non-aggression treaties signed by Adolf Hitler . . . not worth the paper they are printed on!

The cost of weapons: $800,000 a minute

By Harald Mollerstrom
Associated Press

STOCKHOLM — The nations of the world are spending almost $800,000 a minute on arms, 20-times more than industrialized nations spend to help poorer countries, the Stockholm International Peace Research Institute (SIPRI) said yesterday.

SIPRI Chairman Dr. Frank Barnaby said in releasing the group's 1978 edition of "World Armaments and Disarmament."

Barnaby, who is British, said that annual worldwide military spending was twice as high as the yearly gross national product of the whole of Africa, about the same amount the world spent on...

The United States and the Soviet Union account for more than half the world's military spending. Last year's U.S. defense budget was $98 billion, compared with a CIA estimate of $126 billion for the Soviet Union.

Arms trade in developing nations, the...

The United States ranks first, selling 38 percent of the arms imported by the Third World, followed by the Soviet Union at 34 percent and Britain and France at 9 percent each, Barnaby said.

The Mideast is by far the biggest...

were exporting them to other Third World countries. The institute lists warplanes, missiles, armored vehicles and ships as major weapons.

"Although the total value of the arms involved is quite small, it is yet another example of the increasing..."

U.S. PLANS FIRST JET SALE TO CAIRO, REDUCES ISRAELI ORDER FOR CRAFT; SAUDIS GET 60; DEBATE IS EXPECTED

ARMS BALANCE CITED

Sadat Enters the Enemy Land

Carter to Meet Sadat in Egypt

ISRAELIS INVADE LEBANON; LAND, SEA AND AIR UNITS ARE REPORTED IN ACTION

P.L.O. CALLED TARGET

Objectives of Large Force
Said to Be Installations
Used for Terrorist Raids

By WILLIAM E. FARRELL
Special to The New York Times
JERUSALEM, Wednesday, March 15—.

The fires of war have been ignited in the Middle East and the United States and Russia are supplying the fuel. The nations of the world are spending *almost $800,000 a minute on arms* . . . over $400 billion a year. The U.S. defense budget is almost $100 billion; Russia's over $130 billion. And over 500,000 scientists and researchers are engaged in the arms industry worldwide! Each year the arms race and the number of scientists grows. One can see how this will culminate in the Battle of Armageddon!

**A Change
in
Allegiance**

It must be remembered that Israel even today does not have many friends. Its most powerful friend is the United States. But during the Arab oil embargo, when Americans were standing in line for hours to buy gas ... their loyalty to Israel soon diminished. Bumper stickers began to appear on cars:

FORGET ISRAEL! GIVE US ARAB OIL!

Some may forget that at one time Russia was a friend of Israel! This is evidenced by Russia's vote for the partition of Palestine, to which the Arab nations were strongly opposed, in the fall of 1947.

Now, at this point, Israel badly needs friends. And Antichrist rushes in to offer her the friendship of the 10-nation federation. This treaty he makes was foreseen by the prophet Daniel in Daniel 9:27,

> And he [the Antichrist; "the Prince that shall come" of verse 26] shall establish the treaty ["covenant"] with many [Israel and others] for one week [seven year period].

Undoubtedly Antichrist will be an extremely popular individual. One only has to remember Henry Kissinger as insight. Even though Kissinger was unable to achieve peace, and returned in defeat in March, 1975, popularity polls still showed him even more popular than the President of the United States!

With Antichrist finally being able to bring peace to the Middle East; at least a semblance of peace ... his popularity will soar!

Imagine if today some great personage would rise and almost overnight resolve the Arab-Israel crisis to the satisfaction of everyone. The Arabs would go back to developing their land, and the Israeli army could at least reduce its forces to a few thousand . . . what a triumphal victory for the negotiator!

Like a Heaven on Earth

That's what Antichrist will be able to achieve. He will be a brilliant diplomat but also a superb strategist in the art of war.

His rise in power will be sudden and his popularity will be just as sudden. In today's TV age world leaders can be given immediate popularity overnight. Within a few seconds of its occurring, their exploits of victory are transmitted worldwide via the video screen!

The world will become very enthusiastic about his reign. Indeed some marvelous things may be produced at that time. Great new cities may be built and science may make some startling discoveries.

If you live during the reign of Antichrist . . . don't be fooled by his message of peace . . . for his main purpose is to bring a reign of death and destruction.

This will be an era of false security. It will last just 3½ years . . . the first 3½ years of the 7-year Tribulation Period.

By the middle of the Tribulation Period, Israel will have fully served Antichrist's usefulness. He wielded Israel friendship only to serve his own ends . . . those ends

**Antichrist
Becomes
Dictator**

were to make him a world leader. Now, that Antichrist is looked upon as the world leader, all-powerful, he no longer needs the so-called alliance with Israel.

And he is antagonized by Israel's growing glory and independence.

So, this man, who at his merest whim, can change the course of nations, will break his treaty with Israel and order their ceremonial worship to their Lord to cease. No longer may they make sacrifices to their God . . . their full allegiance must be to Antichrist who they should regard along with the rest of the world as the Saviour!

It is this step that ushers in the day Israel dies!

Now let's look at the sequence of the events. When does all of this take place?

The Antichrist will make this convenant with the nation Israel at the very beginning of the Tribulation Period. He will come claiming to be the great man of peace and he will guarantee peace for Israel. He appears to make a seven year peace compact involving Israel which he then proceeds to honor for the first 3½ years of the Tribulation (Daniel 9:27).

**The
Treaty
Made**

After the Antichrist as head of the Federated States of Europe secures the land of Palestine for Israel, Russia seems to start her forces working to overtake this land. But Russia will be defeated. Behind the scenes maneuvering will probably take between 2 and 3 years during the first 3½ year segment of this Tribulation Period.[3]

---

[3] For a comprehensive description of the events that lead up to the Tribulation Period and the Tribulation Period itself, we suggest you read GUIDE TO SURVIVAL by Salem Kirban. $4.95.

19

WHY GOD ALLOWS
THE TRIBULATION PERIOD TO OCCUR

Warnings
Go
Unheeded

Israel had been warned that this Tribulation event would occur. In the Old Testament, these prophecies were predicted in Isaiah, Daniel, and Jeremiah.

Even the Lord Jesus, Himself, had told what was coming and what the Jews would do at that time.

> I am come in my Father's name, and ye receive me not; if another shall come in his own name, him ye will receive (John 5:43).

Let's look at the comparison. Jesus had come without deception, claiming to be sent by His Father.

> For I came down from heaven, not to do mine own will, but the will of him that sent me. (38)

> And this is the Father's will which hath sent me, that of all which He hath given me I should lose nothing, but should raise it up again at the last day (39) (John 6:38-39).

He gave all the glory to His Father.

> And, behold, one came and said unto him,

*Good Master, what good thing shall I do,
that I may have eternal life? (16)*

*And he said unto him, Why callest thou me
good? there is none good but one, that is,
God: but if thou wilt enter into life, keep the
commandments (17) (Matthew 19:16-17).*

*But if I do, though ye believe not me, be-
lieve the works: that ye may know, and
believe, that the Father is in me, and I in
him (John 10:38).*

And yet, Jesus warned the Jews that there
would be one coming who would claim to
be God and demand worship as such.

**It is during this second 3 1/2 year period of
the Tribulation, this man of sin, Antichrist, will be revealed.**

Antichrist
Will Be
Revealed

He is the incarnation of Satan himself.

*And his power shall be mighty, but not by
his own power: and he shall destroy wonderfully, and shall prosper, and practise,
and shall destroy the mighty and the holy
people (Daniel 8:24).*

This will be Satan's supreme effort.

*Therefore rejoice, ye heavens, and ye that
dwell in them. Woe to the inhabiters of the
earth and of the sea! for the devil is come
down unto you, having great wrath, because he knoweth that he hath but a short
time (Revelation 12:12).*

And for this he had schemed thousands of
years.

*How art thou fallen from heaven, O Lucifer
(Satan), son of the morning! how art thou
cut down to the ground, which didst
weaken the nations! (12)*

*For thou hast said in thine heart, I will
ascend into heaven, I will exalt my throne*

above the stars of God: I will sit also upon the mount of the congregation, in the sides of the north: (13)

I will ascend above the heights of the clouds; I will be like the most High (14) (Isaiah 14:12-14).

You will recall that under God's direction Solomon's Temple had been erected upon Mount Moriah. And at the time of dedication, the glory of God had filled this temple with a cloud. It was here that Jehovah had put His name and received worship as the one true God of Israel.

Actually it was to Israel alone that God had revealed Himself in a special way.

We are thine: thou never barest rule over them; they were not called by thy name (Isaiah 63:19).

20

HOW WILL PEOPLE BE SAVED AFTER THE RAPTURE?

No Saved Individual Left

Immediately after the Rapture of the believers (the Christians), there will not be *one single individual on earth who with true saving faith acknowledges Jesus Christ as his personal Saviour and Lord.*

Those left on earth will be those who have not trusted in God's way of salvation. This will start the Tribulation Period of 7 years. It will be one of the darkest hours for man left on earth.

But God's message of salvation will be made known to them. And 7 years later . . .

So many people who have lived during the Tribulation Period will be saved (accept Christ as Lord), that the Bible says they will form

a great multitude
which no man could number
of all nations
kindreds (tribes)
and tongues (languages) — Revelation
7:9-10

Think of it! What a harvest of souls. Seven

years before . . . not one person a Christian . . . but at the end of seven years those saved comprise a multitude which NO MAN COULD NUMBER!

Holy Spirit to Work

After the Rapture occurs, there are no believers. Therefore there are no true Christian missionaries; there are no truly born-again ministers nor evangelists.

And while at the Rapture (taking up of the believers) the Holy Spirit's dwelling in the believers has been removed from the earth . . . He will still be in the world just as He was in Old Testament times before Pentecost. People will be saved during the Tribulation . . . precisely as people were saved during the Old Testament times.

These first believers after the Rapture will be severely persecuted. Quite possibly they will be converted Jews (Matthew 25:40). Few will listen to them (2 Thessalonians 2:1-12) and many of them will die for their testimony and become martyrs.

The 144,000

However, God supernaturally, places His seal on 144,000 Israelites; 12,000 from each of the 12 tribes of Israel. This is described in Revelation 7:3-8. We are told in verse 3 that this seal guarantees their safety and freedom from harm from God's judgments which fall in the Tribulation Period.

While Jews today may not know their tribal lineage, God does and that is what is important . . . and He will reveal it in His time.

Two witnesses will testify from Jerusalem (Revelation 11:5-6). They will perform miracles for 3½ years during the Tribulation Period. They will then be killed but rise again in 3½ days!

Now keep in mind, right now, there are Jews in every part of the world. Actually in every nation and in every language we find physical descendants of Abraham. Those who are part of the 144,000 will be able to immediately witness in their area without going to language school. They will know the culture and language as well as knowing the people.

Near the beginning of the Tribulation Period God will set these 144,000 apart for this special evangelistic ministry. These 144,000 will spread to the world the message of the gospel of salvation by grace through faith.

Because Antichrist will be successful in bringing a semblance of peace in this initial 3½ years of the Tribulation . . . relatively few out of the world's *billions* will pay attention to the 144,000. Quite possibly, the shock of the Rapture will be soon forgotten, and these witnesses will be ridiculed and laughed at.

The
Two
Witnesses

Then also, during the 7 year Tribulation Period God will call TWO WITNESSES (Revelation 11:3-7). These witnesses are raised up to testify mightily for God at this time. They will doubtlessly spur forward the missionary work of the 144,000.

For 3½ years these Two Witnesses will testify—perhaps from Jerusalem. They will be able to perform miracles not only to protect themselves from harm but also to destroy by fire those who oppose their ministry (Revelation 11:5-6).

When the Seal, Trumpet and Vial judgments occur during the 7 years of the Tribulation Period . . . many at this time will realize these are judgments of God . . . and will by the witness of the 144,000, accept the Lord Jesus Christ as their personal Saviour.

At the end of the 3½ year period of the Two Witnesses' ministry, Revelation 11 tells us that God will allow them to be killed and their bodies will lay exposed in the streets of Jerusalem for 3½ days. At the end of the 3½ days, they will rise and ascend to Heaven to the amazement of everyone. Read Revelation 11:11.

Three Groups of Believers Saved

Thus, in the Tribulation Period, we note that the Bible describes at least three groups of believers who will be saved. They are as follows:

1. **EARLY MARTYRS**

   Those who are saved and martyred during the first half of the Tribulation (Revelation 6:9-11).

2. **144,000 FROM ISRAEL**

   These 144,000 Jews are saved by God's supernatural intervention. They are sealed, protected from all harm from God's judgments, and they appear to enter into the Millennium physically preserved (Revelation 7 and 14).

3. **GREAT MULTITUDE FROM ALL NATIONS**

   These are the "great multitude, which no man could number" who are saved much because of the witnessing of the 144,000. They are martyred during the Tribulation

Period (Revelation 7:9-14).

The 144,000 servants of God are sealed in their foreheads. Antichrist, the great imitator, will also cause his followers to receive "a mark in their right hand, or in their foreheads" (Revelation 13:16).

21

THE MARK OF ALLEGIANCE

THE MARK OF THE BEAST (Antichrist)

A Decree
That Brings
Death

In Revelation 13:15 we read that the False Prophet decrees "... that as many as would not worship the image of the beast (Antichrist) should be killed."

If you will look back at verse 7 of this same chapter you will read:

And it was given unto him to make war with the saints and to overcome them: and power was given him over all kindreds, and tongues, and nations.

It is then further revealed how the Antichrist will try to overcome the saints.

And this is how it will happen. He sets up this great religious system with himself (Antichrist) as its god. And in Revelation 13:16-17 we are told:

And he causeth all, both small and great, rich and poor, free and bond, to receive a mark in their right hand, or in their foreheads: (16)

And that no man might buy or sell, save he

that had the mark, or the name of the beast, or the number of his name. (17)

Impossible to Buy or Sell

Therefore, in that day it will be impossible to buy or sell without this identifying sign either on the back of your hand or on your forehead. When an individual refuses to submit to the authority of the Antichrist and will not allow this mark to be put on his body, he faces the consequences of either starving to death slowly or else being slain by a representative of the then existing government.

We already see the pattern being laid for this. The Social Security number is fast becoming the universal number in buying a car, in being admitted to a hospital, in securing a loan, etc. The privilege of buying gas on a certain day during the oil shortage depended on whether you had an odd or an even license plate number.

Identifying the Mark

What this identifying mark will be . . . the Lord has not desired to make clear to us at this time. Nor can we know at this time the identity of Antichrist.

It may be the number **"666"** which is the number of MAN and stops short of the perfect number 7. Thus **"666"** may well represent the humanistic and sinful counterfeit Satanic Trinity falling short of the divine 777, and catering to lost and fallen man. You will recall man was created on the *sixth* day, and in Daniel 3:1-7 we read where Nebuchadnezzar's image to be worshipped was sixty cubits in height, six cubits wide and six instruments of music summoned the worshippers to worship it.

Or, it may be that Antichrist's name or title may add up to a total equalling **"666"** using the following ancient number code (this code could be applied to any alphabetical language):

A =	1	F =	6	K = 20	P =	70	U	= 300
B =	2	G =	7	L = 30	Q =	80	V	= 400
C =	3	H =	8	M = 40	R =	90	W	= 500
D =	4	I =	9	N = 50	S =	100	X	= 600
E =	5	J	= 10	O = 60	T =	200	Y	= 700
							Z	= 800

The author has received letters from many people speculating on who Antichrist might be. Numbers have been juggled to show that it might be the Pope or a world leader.

Another Observation

Rev. Richard Thomas of Ohio suggested that the computer may well become the mechanical monster Antichrist may use to exercise control over the population. In studying this, he came up with the following:

If the number 7 represents perfection, and the number 6 represents imperfection, what if . . .

A =	6	F = 36	K = 66	P =	96	U	= 126
B =	12	G = 42	L = 72	Q =	102	V	= 132
C =	18	H = 48	M = 78	R =	108	W	= 138
D =	24	I = 54	N = 84	S =	114	X	= 144
E =	30	J = 60	O = 90	T =	120	Y	= 150
						Z	= 156

Using this numbering system we find the following

C	=	18
O	=	90
M	=	78
P	=	96
U	=	126
T	=	120
E	=	30
R	=	108
COMPUTER	=	666

This certainly is an interesting observation and time will tell. The computer should play a major role in controlling the population. We are seeing how our lives are already, in part, controlled by computers.

Those people who do carry this mark will most likely prefer to have it on the back of their right hand so that it can readily be seen in the act of signing checks and buying.

It is conceivable that the daily papers will contain a list of the names of those who have been killed the day before who have refused to have this mark imprinted on their forehead or on their hand. According to Revelation 20:4, the instrument of death would seem to be the guillotine, or some similar beheading agent.

With the reign of terror which demands that everyone wear the identifying mark of the Antichrist, and with plague judgments

An Israeli mother weeps over her son's grave as Israeli soldiers prepare
to fight again in a bloodier war.

of the Lord, there will be a mass exodus in which the Jews will try to flee from this destruction into what to them will be unfamiliar and unfriendly territory.

**Flee
To
Petra**

Some Bible scholars believe the area they will flee to is the city of Petra. Others suggest a flight into the wilderness of the nations of the world.

GOD'S PLAN FOR TOMORROW

Here are the future events that will occur in the sequence they will occur:

1. RAPTURE
   When Believers meet Christ in the sky. No future prophecy needs to be fulfilled. The Rapture can occur any hour, any day.
   (I Thessalonians 4:13-18)

2. TRIBULATION PERIOD
   7 years of time when Antichrist and the False Prophet reign and cause world disaster. It is a period of judgment and tribulation on the earth. The Battle of Armageddon occurs at the very end of the Tribulation Period.
   (Daniel 9:27; Matthew 24:21)

3. MILLENNIUM (1000) Reign of Christ
   When all the believers of all the ages reign with Christ. Here on earth the Old Testament promised Kingdom prophecies of world peace will at last come true.
   (Isaiah 11)

4. THE FINAL TEST FOR THOSE ON EARTH
   When Satan for a brief period at the close of the 1000 years has a last opportunity to deceive people and is thrown into the Lake of Fire forever.
   (Revelation 20:7-10)

5. GREAT WHITE THRONE JUDGMENT
   When the unsaved, non-believers, are judged before God and condemned forever to the Lake of Fire. Both living and dead unsaved are judged here. Those previously dead, up to this point, have already been in hell in torment, awaiting this final Judgment Day.
   (Revelation 20:11-15)

6. EARTH BURNS UP
   To purify this earth God sets it afire with a fervent heat.
   (II Peter 3:7,10)

7. THE NEW HEAVEN AND THE NEW EARTH
   All Christians finally reach the ultimate in glory reigning forever with Christ in a new heaven and a new, purged, earth.
   (Revelation 21)

This briefly is the sequence of events. After the Tribulation Period ends, the 1000 year Millennium begins. This is explained in the next chapter.

WHAT AN INHERITANCE!

Life in the Millennium

All of the wonderful things which man has vainly sought in his own strength, without God, will at last be poured out in the kingdom of His Son during the 1000 year MILLENNIUM.

With Satan imprisoned during this time (Revelation 20:1-7) . . . the Millennium Period will be one of

1. PEACE

   Because there will be no war, nations will not have to devote a great part of their budget to war materials. There will be an economic prosperity such as never before has been experienced.

   (Isaiah 11:6-9)

   Perhaps the most well-known verse in relation to this is: And He shall judge between the nations, and shall decide (disputes) for many people; and they shall beat their swords into plowshares, and their spears into pruning hooks; nation shall not lift up sword against nation, neither shall they learn war any more.

   (Isaiah 2:4 Amplified Bible)

   Many political leaders use this verse referring to the goals of this present world. However this verse refers to the MILLENNIUM 1000 YEAR AGE . . . not to this present age.

2. HAPPINESS
   This will be the fulfillment of happiness because there will be
   no more war nor will there be the multitude of sorrows now
   present to man on this earth.

   (Revelation 20:3; Isaiah 11:6-9)

   Therefore with joy will you draw water from the wells of
   salvation.

   (Isaiah 12:3 Amplified Bible)

3. LONG LIFE AND HEALTH
   Here in the 1000 year Millennial Period both sickness and death
   will be well nigh removed. Death will not be banished completely, however, during this period. Open sin may cause some
   to die because the Millennial Period, while filled with multiple
   blessings is still not the end of God's final judgments.

   (Isaiah 65:20)

   Keep these things in mind, however:

   A. The DEFORMED will be HEALED
      And in that day shall the deaf hear the words of the book,
      and out of obscurity and gloom and darkness the eyes
      of the blind shall see."
      (Isaiah 29:18 Amplified Bible; also read Isaiah 35:5, 6)

   B. SICKNESS will be REMOVED
      And no inhabitant will say, I am sick. . . .
      (Isaiah 33:24 Amplified Bible)

   C. SEXUAL REPRODUCTION will EXIST
      Those saints who live through the Tribulation Period
      and enter the 1000 MILLENNIUM in their natural bodies
      will be able to have children throughout this 1000 year
      age. In fact the population of the earth will increase
      rapidly.

      But it must be kept in mind that those who are born
      DURING the 1000 year Millennial Age will have a sin
      nature and it WILL be necessary for them to accept
      Christ if they are to participate in the final and con-
      tinuing eternity that begins after this 1000 year period.

      Here are two more verses to help you understand this
      wonderful blessing:

      Out of them shall come songs of thanksgiving and the
      voices of those who make merry. And I will multiply
      them, and they shall not be few; I will also glorify them,
      and they shall not be small.

      Their children too shall be as in former times. . . .
      (Jeremiah 30:19,20 Amplified Bible)

4. PROSPERITY
   The Millennium Period will be one of unequalled prosperity.
   There will be such an abundance that there will be no want.

   Perhaps the most familiar verse . . . and one we hear quoted as
   referring to today . . . is the verse below, which refers to the
   1000 year MILLENNIUM PERIOD:
   > The wilderness and the dry land shall be glad, the desert
   > shall rejoice and blossom as the rose and the autumn
   > crocus.
   > It shall blossom abundantly, and rejoice even with joy and
   > singing; the glory of Lebanon shall be given to it, the excel-
   > lency of Mount Carmel and the plain of Sharon. . . .
   >> (Isaiah 35:1,2 Amplified Bible)

   Here will be a desert that will have all the glory of Lebanon
   given to it! The glory of Lebanon is found in the strength and
   statelines of its cedars. The excellency of Carmel and Sharon,
   which consisted of corn and cattle, will likewise then charac-
   terize this transformed desert!

5. A JOY IN LABOR
   Under the direction of Christ there will be a perfect economic
   system in which people will work in complete joy and desire
   to provide the necessities of life.
   > They shall build houses and inhabit them, and they shall plant
   > vineyards and eat the fruit of them . . . My chosen and elect
   > shall long make use of and enjoy the work of their hands.
   >> (Isaiah 65:21,22 Amplified Bible)

6. LANGUAGE WILL BE PURE
   In this blessed period language will not be used for taking
   God's name in vain or for other wrong pruposes. Lips will
   glorify and praise God. Perhaps the language of the earth will
   at this time be unified.

   > For then I will give to the people a clear and pure speech
   > from pure lips . . .
   >> (Zephaniah 3:9)

7. GOD WILL BE PRESENT
   This will be a time when we can fellowship with God and
   enjoy His manifested presence in a special way.
   > My tabernacle or dwelling place also shall be with them;
   > and I will be their God. . . .

   > The abode of God is with men, and He will live among
   > them, and they shall be His people and God shall personally
   > be with them and be their God.
   >> (Ezekiel 37:27, Revelation 21:3 Amplified Bible)

22

THE FINAL CURTAIN

Surviving
The
Tribulation

What happens to the Christians who are living during the Tribulation Period and survive . . . still being alive when it is time for the 1000 year Millennial Age to be ushered in by Christ?

And also, what happens to the non-believers who are living during the Tribulation and survive the Tribulation judgments of God?

Scriptures seem to indicate that although one-third of those on earth during the Tribulation may be killed (Revelation 9:15) . . . still two-thirds will remain. An insight into what occurs then is found in Matthew 25:32-46.

Here we find Christ relating the judgment of the sheep and goats. To the goats; that is to those who have in the Tribulation period rejected Christ by unbelief and who have manifested this by refusing to help Christ's persecuted brethren during this period, our Lord says:

> *Be gone from Me, you cursed, into the eternal fire prepared for the devil and his angels! . . .*
> *Then they will go away into eternal punishment . . . (Matthew 25:41, 46 Amplified Bible)*

To the sheep; that is, those living in the Tribulation period who have manifested a love for Christ by aiding His persecuted brethren, . . . to these will come the invitation:

> *Come, you blessed of my Father, inherit— receive as your own—the kingdom prepared for you from the foundation of the world . . . (Matthew 25:34 Amplified Bible)*

This judgment must occur before Christ begins the 1000 year MILLENNIUM period . . . for the still living non-believers have no right to enter this 1000 year reign with Christ and the saved.

But note the blessed promise for the one who has turned to Christ and who has lived through the Tribulation Period . . . and for Christians of all ages as well. In this last passage Christ is telling you that way back in eternity when the foundations of

**The
1000 Year
Reign**

the world were made . . . this eternal Kingdom was prepared for you.

All of the wonderful things which man has vainly sought in his own strength, without God, will at last be poured out in the kingdom of His Son during the 1000 year MILLENNIUM.

Satan will be imprisoned during this time (Revelation 20:1-7).

The 1000 year Millennium Period will take place *right here* on earth. The earthly center of this Reign with Christ will be in Jerusalem.

The Millennium will not yet be Heaven (compare Isaiah 65:20 with Revelation 21:4 to see this).

It will be a theocracy.

A theocracy is a government in which God is recognized as the supreme civil ruler and His laws are taken as the laws of the state.

And the Lord will choose Jerusalem to be the center of all spiritual blessing.

> And the Lord shall inherit Judah as His portion in the holy land, and shall again choose Jerusalem . . . Yes, many peoples and numerous nations shall come to seek the Lord of hosts at Jerusalem and to entreat favor of the Lord . . .
>
> Everyone that is left of all the nations that came against Jerusalem shall go up from year to year to worship the king, the Lord of Hosts. (Zechariah 2:12; 8:22, 14:16 KJV)

Who will be in the Millennium?

The people will include:

1. *All the saved of Israel alive at the end of the Tribulation Period;*
2. *All the saved of the Gentiles alive at the end of the Tribulation Period (They will have natural bodies in the Millennium Period); plus*
3. *The Believers who have died before the Rapture. These resurrected saints will have positions of responsibility in the Millennium. (Matthew 19:28; Luke 19:12-27)*

(Note: It is only fair to here note that while the Bible teaches that the saints who have believed in Christ and who have died will rule with Christ in the 1000 year Millennial Kingdom (Matthew 19:28; Revelation 20:6), yet many excellent Bible teachers believe that this will be a reign in Heaven and not on the Millennial earth. The Bible is clear that they will indeed reign! Whether in Heaven or earth is certainly a lesser question. From Matthew 19:28, amazing as it may sound, it does in fact *appear* that the resurrected believers will actually reign on earth with Christ during the 1000 years.)

Resurrected Believers and Living Believers . . . The DIFFERENCE!

In our context the living believers are those who are still alive at the time the Millennium Period is ushered in right after the Tribulation. These have survived the Tribulation Period.

These living believers, during the Millennium 1000 year period, will marry and be given in marriage. The women will reproduce and have children. These believers will have natural bodies!

THREE VIEWS ON THE MILLENNIUM

THE MILLENNIUM POSITIONS	WHAT DOES IT MEAN	WHAT EACH GROUP BELIEVES	OBJECTION OR SUPPORT
POST MILLENNIALISM	Christ will come to establish His Kingdom on Earth AFTER (Post) the 1000 Years (Millennium).	The earth will get better and better through the spread of the Gospel, and Christ will come to claim His Kingdom after 1000 years of peace has transpired.	Naïve. The earth is not getting better; and the Bible does not teach that it is (II Timothy 3:1-7).
A MILLENNIALISM	There will be NO FUTURE Earthly 1000 year Reign (Millennium). (In Greek "A" at the beginning of a word means "NO.")	The Millennium is *NOW!* Peace on earth exists in the Church; and Satan is NOW bound so that he cannot prevent the spread of the Gospel.	Revelation 20:3 says that Satan goes to prison "that he should deceive the nations no more." Look at Cuba, China and Russia. Satan is not NOW in prison.
PRE MILLENNIALISM	Christ will come personally to judge the wicked and to establish His Kingdom BEFORE (Pre) the 1000 years (Millennium) begins.	The earth is getting worse, and the Kingdom age cannot begin until Christ comes to destroy the wicked.	This is the teaching of the Bible. Christ will come (Revelation 19: 11-21) and then the Kingdom will be set up (Revelation 20).

THESE POSITIONS HAVE *NOTHING* TO DO WITH THE SALVATION OF A SINNER.

But what about the saints who died and those who were living on the earth immediately prior to the Tribulation Period? These saints—called the _resurrected believers_—meet Christ in the air at the RAPTURE!

They are given heavenly bodies and Scripture tells us that they:

> _Which shall be accounted worthy to obtain that world (heaven), and the resurrection from the dead, neither marry, nor are given in marriage:_
>
> _Neither can they die any more: for they are equal unto the angels; and are the children of God. . . . (Luke 20:35, 36 KJV)_

Therefore, during the 1000 year Millennium Reign with Christ there will exist, it appears, two classes of believers, having two different bodies:

> The _Living_ Believers—in natural bodies.
> The _Resurrected_ Believers—in glorified resurrection bodies.

The Final Temple

In the Millennial 1000 year age . . . the final TEMPLE will apparently be built in Jerusalem. There will, however, be NO TEMPLE built by man's hands in the New Heaven and New Earth which follows the Millennium.

The Decision

Remember now, while all those at the very beginning of the 1000 year Millennium are believers . . . there are people born during the Millennium to the living saints who endured the Tribulation Period. And each of those born during the Millennial Period will have to individually decide either to accept Christ or reject Him. But for the Christian, he will live 1000 years and in eternity he will dwell forever in a land where he'll never grow old!

Some will reject Him! This is possible because sin will still be possible during this 1000 years! In Zechariah 14:17-19 we are told that certain families and certain nations will refuse "to go up to Jerusalem to worship before the Lord."

And this will usher in . . . at the end of the 1000 year Millennium Period . . . Satan's final folly!

Satan's Big Moment Arrives

The final stage for Satan has been set. Just one more time . . . that's all he asks . . . just one more time to achieve his sinful goals.

It appears that those who will be deceived when Satan is once again loosed will be some of the children born during this Millennial Age.

And here is the tragedy!

> . . . when the thousand years are expired, Satan shall be loosed out of his prison,
> And shall go out to deceive the nations which are in the four quarters of the earth, Gog and Magog, to gather them together to battle: the number of whom is as the sand of the sea. (Revelation 20:7, 8 KJV)

Millions Follow Satan

THINK OF IT! Satan will gather an army so big . . . the number of whom is as the sand of the sea.

After living in 1000 years of prosperity, wealth, without sickness and very little death, with an abundance of everything

. . . SOME ARE STILL NOT SATISFIED. And Satan deceives them into believing he can offer them something better! And so clever is his deception that he musters an army AS NUMEROUS AS THE SAND OF THE SEA!

Read that over again! Can you imagine . . . after living 1000 years in a Golden Age . . . fathom this? What a heartache God must have and what patience with mortal man!

Is it no wonder that the NEW HEAVEN and NEW EARTH do not begin until this final weeding out of the chaff is accomplished!

Now, perhaps you can understand why Satan is once again let loose . . . for there is waiting a host of people to join him—a host as numerous as the sand of the sea!

How much sand is there in the sea? Well, this might help you visualize the vastness of Satan's following. The sea occupies 70.8% of the surface of the earth! And with much of the sea's shore and bottom surface covered with sand . . . those that join Satan must represent a very large group . . . yet they probably represent only a minority of the Millennial Kingdom.

One may wonder where all the people come from! However, it must be kept in mind that during the 1000 year Millennial reign—war, suffering and even death will have been held in check and mankind will multiply profusely. And with God blessing the ground to give an abundant harvest the earth will be able to support such a large population.

Thus, we see the ingratitude and blindness of millions who have tasted for a thousand years the blessings of Heaven . . . but as soon as they can escape this authority . . . they rush to the folly of Satan.

Gog and Magog Defined

You will recall that in the last Scripture verse we quoted (Revelation 20:8) there was a reference to the nations of Gog and Magog joining Satan.

This can be confusing to the new Christian since these same names, Gog and Magog, appear in Ezekiel 39:1, 2.

> In Ezekiel, Gog of the country of Magog refers to the great enemy of the North who shall rush toward Palestine before or during the Tribulation 7 years. Most evangelicals believe this is Russia.

> However, in Revelation 20:8, this mention of Gog and Magog refers to those who from the *four corners of the earth* (not just Russia) let themselves be led in the last battle against God.

> **The event mentioned in Revelation 20:8 occurs at the end of the 1000 year MILLENNIUM Period.**

It must be kept in mind that the rebellion of Satan and his followers does *not* occur in the 1000 year Millennial Period, but rather, it *follows* it!

> *And when the thousand years are expired, Satan shall be loosed. . . . (Revelation 20:7 KJV)*

And as in previous history that will have long since passed . . . Satan's prime attack will again be directed against the believers (of Christ) and His city, Jerusalem!

The Scriptures tell us:

> And they (Satan and his army) swarmed up over the broad plain of the earth and encircled the fortress (camp) of God's people (the saints) and the beloved city (Jerusalem)....(Revelation 20:9 Amplified Bible).

It is not difficult to understand why Satan first wants to strike Jerusalem. Driven from Heaven long before, Satan is anxious to strike at the heart of God's throne and sanctuary.

But though Satan gathers his rebel following "to battle," there is no battle!

What occurs next—the most tragic occurrence beyond the scope of man's wildest finite imagination—brings an end to Satan's final folly!

The Final War

With all his men, more numerous than the sands of the sea, one would think Satan would make some dent in his invasion of the area around Jerusalem.

And, were it not for God . . . he could and would. But something unusual occurs!

God causes a spectacular phenomenon to take place.

Here's how the Bible describes it:

> . . . fire came down from God out of Heaven, and devoured them! (Revelation 20:9 KJV)

Think of it! Multiple thousands, in fact millions of people, in a flashing moment, are suddenly consumed by fire that came

THE RESURRECTIONS

Heaven

Paradise

Judgment Seat of Christ

Great White Throne

Resurrection of the Dead Unbelievers
Revelation 20:11-13; Jude 6

"And whosoever was not found written in the Book of Life was cast into the Lake of Fire."
Revelation 20:15

Unbelievers cast into Lake of Fire eternally

"And I saw the dead, small and great, stand before God; and the books were opened: and another book was opened, which is the book of life: and the dead were judged out of those things which were written in the books, according to their works.
And the sea gave up the dead which were in it; and death and hell delivered up the dead which were in them: and they were judged every man according to their works."
Revelation 20:12-13

Marriage of the Lamb
Revelation 19:7-9

Christ Returns to Earth with His Saints
1 Thessalonians 3:13; Zechariah 14:4

"For we must all appear before the judgment seat of Christ....."
2 Corinthians 5:10
Believers now in New Bodies
Philippians 3:20-21

Resurrection of Tribulation Saints
Daniel 12:1-2

Believers meet with Christ in the air
1 Thessalonians 4:16

"....the dead in Christ shall rise First...."
"Then we which are alive and remain shall be caught up together with them in the clouds to meet the Lord in the air....." 1 Thessalonians 4:16-17

Believers who have died before the Rapture. Present in a celestial, spiritual body.*

"And Jesus said unto him, Verily I say unto thee, To-day shalt thou be with me in paradise."
Luke 23:43

"We are confident, I say, and willing rather to be absent from the body, and to be present with the Lord."
2 Corinthians 5:8

Resurrection and Ascension of Christ into Heaven
(Matthew 27:52-53 tells of others who were resurrected after Christ—these were the wave-sheaf of the harvest to come. Leviticus 23:10-11.)

Acts 1:1-11
Matthew 27:50-53

*Physical body remains in grave awaiting Rapture

About A.D. 30	This Present Age	A.D.?	Rapture	Seven Year Tribulation Period	Mount of Olives Armageddon	1000 Year Millennial Age	With Satan Antichrist and False Prophet

thundering down from Heaven. Sounds unbelievable, doesn't it?

At this point all the unsaved are dead!

So Satan's ambitions, generated sometime early in the earth's beginnings and nurtured through all time until the end of the 1000 year Millennial Period . . . are finally once and for all CRUSHED by God. In one swift judgment—related in the English Bible in just 12 short words—in just one-third of one Scripture verse God, in effect says to Satan's ambitions, "Satan, THIS IS THE END!"

12 words crush Satan's hopes:

> . . . and fire came down from God out of Heaven, and devoured them. (Revelation 20:9 KJV)

The Final Judgment

What happens next?

Is Satan dead? Are his millions of followers forgotten? No. Their harvest of sin has been sown. Now is the time they will reap their "rewards."

First God takes care of Satan whose deception caused millions to abandon Christ.

> And the devil (Satan) that deceived them was cast into the lake of fire and brimstone, where the beast (Antichrist) and the false prophet are, and shall be tormented day and night for ever and ever. (Revelation 20:10 KJV)

There are some who will read this passage and laugh. "Thrown into the lake of fire . . . what a fairy tale . . . an allegory . . . surely a God of love could not do this . . . and how

can one be tormented day and night forever and ever?"

Perhaps you, as mere man, don't believe.
But think about this for a moment. Satan
and his angels believe! Turn to James 2:19

> ... the devils also believe and tremble.
> (James 2:19 KJV)

If Satan and his angels believe ... and in
believing ... tremble ... should you any
less believe that when God says something
... He means it!

Satan is thus judged and cast into the lake
of fire with Antichrist and the False
Prophet who have already been there a
1000 years.

Now comes the most tragic moment of this
world.

> Then I saw a great white throne and the
> One Who was seated upon it, from Whose
> presence and from the sight of Whose face
> earth and sky fled away and no place was
> found for them. (Revelation 20:11
> Amplified Bible)

Apparently the awesomeness of this occa-
sion is so tragic it is hard for anyone to
fully comprehend ... "the earth and sky"
even flee from it.

The unsaved dead are then raised from the
dead in what is commonly referred to as
the "second resurrection" (the first resurrection being when the believers were
raised to life eternal with Christ)—
(Revelation 20:5-14).

Then—the saddest verse of all:

> And whosoever was not found written in
> the book of life was cast into the lake of fire.
> (Revelation 20:15 KJV)

This is the final curtain for Satan, for Antichrist, for the False Prophet and for the millions who through the ages rejected Christ as their personal Saviour and Lord! For them, it is a night that never ends!

A
Fresh
Start . . .
Earth
Purified!

Now God desires to wipe the slate entirely clean from every trace of sin . . . and He is going to do it by purging the earth by fire . . . giving His saints a New Heaven and a New Earth.

The Bible tells us:

> . . . the heavens will pass away with a roar
> and the elements will be destroyed with
> intense heat, and the earth and all its
> works will be burned up. (2 Peter 3:10 ASV)

The Earth will be burned with fire . . . and fire acts as a purifier in its melting process which does not diminish the totality of earth's matter but simply gives it a new form. Thus the world is purified from the contamination of sin and is surrounded by a new atmosphere, new heavens, and will become the residence of the righteous.

23

THE DAY THAT NEVER ENDS

**The
Glorious
Sequel**

There is no chapter that gives me a greater thrill to write than this one. The event that we will now describe will fulfill all of the aspirations of the Old Testament saints, of the New Testament saints and of the Tribulation and Millennial saints.

No earthly pen can hope to convey the completeness of joy and the fullness of peace that will be ours as Christians, born-again believers, in God's New Heaven and New Earth!

But some day, God will reveal our Heavenly inheritance and it will be beyond human words . . .

> The false and empty shadows
> The life of sin, are past—
> God gives me mine inheritance,
> The land of life at last.

**The
New Heavens
and
New Earth**

There will be no homesickness for the old things of Earth—such will be the dazzling splendor of this New Earth!

As we mentioned previously the New

Heaven and New Earth do *not* come into being until

1. *After the battle of Armageddon (Revelation 19)*
2. *After the Millennial reign of Christ (Revelation 20)*
3. *After the judgment of sinners at the Great White Throne (Revelation 20)*
4. *After the present earth is burned up (II Peter 3; Revelation 21)*

**Our
New
Body**

Scriptures indicate that we will be the same person having the same soul as we now have. We will also have a new glorified body.

The characteristics of this new body will no doubt bear a relationship to our former body much the same as the qualities of Christ's resurrection body bore to His same pre-resurrection body.

The Bible tells us that when we accept Christ as Saviour and Lord we too are spiritually a new creation:

> . . . *if any man be in Christ, he is a new creature; old things are passed away; behold, all things are become new. (II Corinthians 5:17 KJV)*

All will be new in that day . . . New Heavens, New Earth, and New Jerusalem (Revelation 21:1, 2).

Here will be a place finally without corruption. No decay, no rust. Many people today think that silver won't rust, but rust, which is iron-oxide, also has its counterpart even in silver-oxide and silver-sulfide. All metals today corrode in one way or another. As an example, for every hour of plane flight in Vietnam, it required 25 man-hours of anti-corrosion maintenance. NASA and the military together spend $6 billion per year fighting corrosion damage even in peace time!

God tells us:

> Your gold and silver is cankered; and the rust of them shall be a witness against you ....(James 5:3 KJV)

Thus, believers, who through acceptance of Christ, are now new creatures, will be completely fulfilled in all of God's glory in the New Heavens and the New Earth.

You will recall that the relationship between Christ and His saints is revealed in Christ's prayer of intercession in Gethsemane when He prayed:

> Father, I will that they also, whom thou hast given me, be with me where I am; that they may behold my glory, which thou hast given me. . . . (John 17:24 KJV)

NO Temple

It is hard for man to fathom the characteristics of this New City, Jerusalem. It is also an eternal city WITHOUT a Temple!

You will recall that there will be a Temple in the Millennial earth. But here in the New City, Jerusalem, there will be no need for a Temple. Christ will be that Temple. The entire city will be that Temple—a vast cubical (Revelation 21:16) Holy of Holies wherein God dwells. Since there will be no sin and our conversation and thoughts will be holy we will be dwelling with God in that Holy City.

**NO
NIGHT**

There will be no night there. Christ will be the light that illumines that City.

> . . . I am the light of the world: he that followeth me shall not walk in darkness, but shall have the light of life. (John 8:12 KJV)

With sin gone and with the saints being in the physical presence of God His light will be our light and there will be no night there.

> . . . for there shall be no night there. (Revelation 21:25 KJV)

**NO TEARS
NO DEATH**

There will be no more tears in Heaven. There will be no more pain in Heaven. There will be no more sorrow, no crying in Heaven. There will be no more death in Heaven! Hear God's promises to every Christian who has placed his faith and trust in Him:

> . . . God shall wipe away all tears from their eyes; and there shall be no more death, neither sorrow, nor crying, neither shall there be any more pain: FOR THE FORMER THINGS ARE PASSED AWAY. (Revelation 21:4 KJV)

What a glorious transformation . . . when His blessed face I see . . . no more pain and no more sorrow . . . O what glory that will be!

**NO
More
Separation**

All the saints of all the ages will be there. No more will friends have to part again. No more will families have to have tearful farewells. What a grand reunion saints in

And He carried me away in the Spirit to a great and high mountain, and showed me the holy city, Jerusalem, coming down out of heaven from God (Revelation 21:10).

Christ will enjoy forever and forever. As Dr. Wilbur M. Smith has so wonderfully reminded us . . . there will be no need to carry photographs of our absent loved ones in order for us to renew our memory of them . . . for those who have been absent for years . . . will now be ever present. No more disagreements, or misunderstandings, with our loved ones. Together, the believers will rejoice in everlasting joy and companionship.

ONLY
For The
Redeemed

No unsaved person will be in Heaven . . . nothing that would defile this Heavenly Kingdom. How true that old things will have passed away and all things will then be new!

As Dr. J. Dwight Pentecost has so excellently pointed out in his fine book, THINGS TO COME, life in that eternal city of the New Jerusalem will include:

1. A life of fellowship with Him
2. A life of rest
3. A life of full knowledge
4. A life of holiness
5. A life of joy
6. A life of service
7. A life of abundance
8. A life of glory
9. A life of worship

What greater promise is there than that found in 1 John:

> . . . we know that when He shall appear, we shall be like Him. . . . (I John 3:2 KJV)

What is Heaven?

Heaven is a place where Mansions have

already been prepared for us:

> In my Father's house are many mansions
> . . . I go to prepare a place for you . . . that
> where I am, there ye may be also. . . . (John
> 14:2, 3 KJV)

**A Place
of
Prepared
Mansions**

Heaven is a place where all our saved loved ones will be:

> Then we which are alive and remain shall
> be caught up together with them [our saved
> loved ones] in the clouds, to meet the Lord
> in the air: and so shall we [all of the saved]
> ever be with the Lord. (I Thessalonians 4:17
> KJV)

Heaven is a place where we shall see God:

> Then we . . . shall be caught up . . . to meet
> the Lord in the air: and so shall we ever be
> with the Lord (I Thessalonians 4:17 KJV)

Heaven is a place where we will have new bodies:

> So also is the resurrection of the dead, It
> [the body] is sown [planted] in corruption;
> it is raised in incorruption. (I Corinthians
> 15:42 KJV)

Heaven is a place where we will receive rewards:

> If any man's work abide which he hath
> built thereupon, he shall receive a reward.
> (I Corinthians 3:14 KJV)

Heaven is a place where we will be given wonderful rewards. The Bible describes these as crowns, wreaths of victory (*stephanos* in the Greek), as those given to the winners of the Grecian games.

However the crowns of the Christian are

eternal, enduring, and golden.

> Now they [those who participate in the Grecian games] do it to obtain a corruptible crown, but we an incorruptible. (I Corinthians 9:25 KJV)

Our Eternal Crowns

Is it not time we realign our priorities in life and place our emphasis on those things that have eternal values? Here are the eternal crowns that await us **tomorrow** . . . if we are faithfully serving Him **today!**

1. A Crown of Life
   > . . . he (the Christian) shall receive the crown of life, which the Lord hath promised to them that love Him. (James 1:12 KJV)

2. A Crown of Righteousness
   > Henceforth there is laid up for me a crown of righteousness, which the Lord, the righteous judge, shall give me at that day: and not to me only, but unto all them also that love His appearing. (II Timothy 4:8 KJV)

3. A Crown of Glory
   > And when the chief Shepherd shall appear, ye shall receive a crown of glory that fadeth not away. (I Peter 5:4)

4. A Crown for Soul Winners
   > For what is our hope, or joy, or crown of rejoicing—is it not even yourselves [Paul's converts]—in the presence of our Lord Jesus at His appearing? (I Thessalonians 2:19 From the Greek)

5. A Crown for Martyrs
   > . . . behold, the devil shall cast some of you into prison . . . be thou faithful unto death, and I will give thee a crown of life. (Revelation 2:10 KJV)

And Christ promises that He will come quickly to call for His own, and He thus urges us in the Scriptures to be strong in the Last Days, not to give in to false doctrine nor to those who would say, "Where is the promise of His coming?" But rather, Christ tells His followers:

> . . . hold that fast which thou hast, that no man take thy crown.

and promises

> Him that overcometh will I make a pillar in the temple of my God. . . . (Revelation 3:11, 12 KJV)

And so overjoyed will we be in this New Jerusalem that we will cast our crowns at His pierced feet (Revelation 4:10).

> And when the battle's over,
> We shall wear a crown!
> We shall wear a crown!
> We shall wear a crown!
> And when the battle's over,
> We shall wear a crown in the New Jerusalem!
> Then we shall be
>   where we would be
> Then we shall be
>   what we should be
> Things that are not now
>   nor could be
> Soon shall be
>   our own!

What joy will be ours, eternally, in the Day that Never Ends!

WHAT WILL YOU DO WITH JESUS?

After reading this book it should become evident to you that the world is not getting better and better.

What happens when it comes time for you to depart from this earth? Then WHAT WILL YOU DO WITH JESUS?

Here are five basic observations in the Bible of which you should be aware:

1. **ALL SIN** — For all have sinned, and come short of the glory of God (Romans 3:23).

2. **ALL LOVED** — For God so loved the world, that He gave His only begotten Son, that whosoever believeth in Him should not perish, but have everlasting life (John 3:16).

3. **ALL RAISED** — Marvel not at this: for the hour is coming, in which all that are in the graves shall hear his voice.

   And shall come forth; they that have done good, unto the resurrection of life; and they that have done evil, unto the resurrection of damnation (John 5:28,29).

4. **ALL JUDGED** — we shall all stand before the judgment seat of Christ (Romans 14:10).

   And I saw the dead, small and great, stand before God; and the books were opened . . . (Revelation 20:12).

5. **ALL BOW** — at the name of Jesus every knee should bow . . . (Philippians 2:10)

Right now, in simple faith, you can have the wonderful assurance of eternal life.

Ask yourself, honestly, the question . . . . WHAT WILL I DO WITH JESUS?

God tells us the following:

   ". . . him that cometh to me I will in no wise cast out. (37) Verily, verily (truly) I say unto you, He that believeth on me (Christ) *hath* everlasting life" (47)—(John 6:37, 47).

He also is a righteous God and a God of indignation to those who reject Him. . . . .

   ". . . he that believeth not is condemned already, because he hath not believed in the name of the only begotten Son of God"—(John 3:18).

   "And whosoever was not found written in the book of life was cast into the lake of fire"—(Revelation 20:15).

YOUR MOST IMPORTANT DECISION IN LIFE

All of your riches here on earth—all of your financial security—all of your material wealth, your houses, your land will crumble into nothingness in a few years.

No matter how great your works—no matter how kind you are—no matter how philanthropic you are—it means nothing in the sight of God, because in the sight of God, your riches are as filthy rags.

". . . all our righteousnesses are as filthy rags . . ." (Isaiah 64:6)

Christ expects you to come as you are, a sinner, recognizing your need of a Saviour, the Lord Jesus Christ.

Understanding this, why not bow your head right now and give this simple prayer of faith to the Lord.

My Personal Decision for CHRIST

"Lord Jesus, I know that I'm a sinner and that I cannot save myself by good works. I believe that you died for me and that you shed your blood for my sins. I believe that you rose again from the dead. And now I am receiving you as my personal Saviour, my Lord, my only hope of salvation. I know that I cannot save myself. Lord, be merciful to me, a sinner, and save me according to the promise of Your Word. I want Christ to come into my heart now to be my Saviour, Lord and Master."

Signed ....

Date ....

If you have signed the above, having just taken Christ as your personal Saviour and Lord . . . I would like to rejoice with you in your new found faith.

Write to me . . . Salem Kirban, Kent Road, Huntingdon, Valley, Penna. 19006 . . . and I'll send you a little booklet to help you start living your new life in Christ.

Use this ORDER FORM to order additional copies of

THE RISE
OF
ANTICHRIST

by Salem Kirban

You will want to give **THE RISE OF ANTICHRIST** to your loved ones and friends.

An excellent book to give to those who want to know how their world is changing and how to prepare for their future . . . for the next 10 years . . . and for an eternity!

PRICES

1 copy: $4.95

3 copies: $12 (You save $2.85)
5 copies: $20 (You save $4.75)

WE PAY POSTAGE!

ORDER FORM

To:

SALEM KIRBAN, Inc.
Kent Road
Huntingdon, Valley, Penna. 19006 U.S.A.

Enclosed find $ _____ for _____ copies of
THE RISE OF ANTICHRIST by Salem Kirban

Ship postage paid to:

Name _____
(Please PRINT)

Street _____

City _____

State _____ Zip Code _____

Order from your local Christian bookstore. If they cannot supply you . . . send $4.95 to:
SALEM KIRBAN, Inc., 2117 Kent Road, Huntingdon Valley, Penna. 19006 U.S.A.

Special Report No.

HUMANISM...
SINISTER, SUBTLE SEDUCTION

Humanism is a deadly philosophy...a philosophy that is often used by Satan to deaden the effectiveness of Christian witness. It is a real threat to the Christian School movement. Yet most believers in Christ have no idea how dangerous Humanism really is!

Humanists do not believe in God. They worship the creature rather than the Creator. They endorse abortion, genetic engineering, day care centers. They seek to break the family unit and its discipline. Distribute this Special Newsletter in your Church and School.

Special Report No.

THE TRILATERIAL COMMISSION
America's New Secret Government

The Trilateral Commission is an extension of the Council on Foreign Relations (CFR). Its ultimate goal is to incorporate Japan, Canada, the United States and the Common Market nations of Europe into a one-world socialistic governmental web.

The name, TRILATERAL, is derived from the fact that the leaders come from three democratic areas of the world...the United States, Western Europe and Japan. David Rockefeller hand-picked this elite group of some 250 individuals to begin this organization. They are world shapers!

Special Report No.

THE POWER SEEKERS...
The Bilderbergers & CFR

The Bilderbergers, the CFR, the Trilateralists all have one thing in common . . . they are secret societies. The Bilderbergers have always been directed by Prince Bernhard of the Netherlands. The Bilderbergers favor an international money system called the "bancor system."

They predicted the recession and many believe both they and the CFR were influential in the control of oil and the rapid price rises of gasoline and heating oils. The CFR seeks an ultimate world order into a united nations. Antichrist will head such a European union!

Special Report No.

THE ILLUMINATI

In recent years in Christian circles there have been hushed whispers about the conspiracy of the IL-LUMINATI. Many believe their aims are to control the world through their arch leader, Satan! This Report traces the history of the ILLUMINATI and it may surprise you!

The Illuminati power structure has infiltrated into the United States, according to some reports. Did the Illuminati engineer both World War 1 and World War 2? And are they now planning World War 3? Is the current Middle East crisis part of this sinister plan?

Special Report No.

HOW THE MONEY MANIPULATORS
KEEP YOU POOR!

We are now living in the Age of ANTICHRIST. One real indication of this is that the United States is now controlled, in large part, by powerful foreign interests.

About 200 years ago, Benjamin Franklin wrote that the conspiracy plan that would develop would be: "... get first all the people's money, then all their lands, and then make them and their children your servants forever!" Reveals why the Federal Reserve is neither Federal nor Reserve! The 6-Point Plan to reduce you to POVERTY!

Special Report No.

THE SATANIC TRINITY EXPOSED

One of these days some great leader, admired by the world as a man of peace, will settle the Arab-Israeli dispute. Watch out when this event happens. For this man will become known as the Antichrist. His sweet words of peace will soon lead to the most devastating seven years of terror.

Antichrist is a part of the Satanic Trinity (just as Christ is part of the Heavenly Trinity). The counterfeit Trinity is Satan, Antichrist and the False Prophet. A revealing study of their strategy, that has already begun!

Special Report No. **7**

WHAT IN THE WORLD WILL HAPPEN NEXT!

As we enter the 1980's, we are abruptly brought face to face with the fact that our world has *"progressed"* so rapidly that our natural resources are at a point of depletion.

The 1980's will witness chaos, confusion, and a frightening world war! This Report tells you exactly what will happen next! Includes easy-to-understand Charts on Bible prophecy. Makes God's promises in Revelation come alive. Clearly outlines God's 14-point program beginning with the Rapture.

Special Report No. **8**

CHARTS ON REVELATION

Daniel and Revelation deal primarily with future events.

Many people have difficulty grasping the dramatic truths found here.

Salem Kirban has taken the prophetic portions of Scripture and designed clear, concise Charts that any person can understand. You will find this Special Report packed with charts and statistics illustrating every phase of the Tribulation, the Millennium and the New Heavens and New Earth. Excellent to give to loved ones!

Special Report No. **9**

WHAT IS HELL LIKE?

How sad that many people spend their entire life preparing for a few years of retirement. We are only alloted 60 to 70 years on earth, yet most of our waking hours are concerned with this small unit of time! We never give thought to eternity.

When asked about one's future, many put off making a decision to accept Christ as personal Saviour and Lord of their life. Procrastination is Satan's most effective tool. This Report details exactly what Hell is like. It also clearly explains how to get to Heaven!

Special Report No. **10**

WHAT IS HEAVEN LIKE?

You hear very few messages preached on Heaven. And very few books are written on this subject. That is why you will find this Special Report so heartwarming.

Heaven is a place where believers will receive a new body. There will be no more death, no more tears, no more separation from loved ones in Christ, no more illness, and no night! But there will be so much more! How will your body differ from your present body? Will you recognize your loved ones? These questions and many more are answered fully!

Special Report No. **11**

WHAT IS THE TRIBULATION LIKE?

The Tribulation Period will unleash a holocaust of horror such as the world has never seen! It will usher in Antichrist and the False Prophet. Everyone will be forced to wear an identifying Mark on their right hand or forehead or they will not be able to buy or sell!

Already we are witnessing the beginning of these sorrows. Events happening right now are preparing us for the Tribulation when every life will be controlled by Government. You owe it to yourself to know exactly what lies ahead in the not too distant future!

Special Report No. **12**

RUSSIA'S RISE TO RUIN!

The saddest fact about Russia's rise in these Last Days is that she will destroy the independent status of the United States and force us to join the Common Market nations as an European conglomerate! Such a move will, of course, usher in the rise of Antichrist.

Now! You can follow Russia's path of conquest through this Special Report. Watch as she topples country after country with her final aim the destruction of Israel and the control of Mid-East oil fields. A revealing study. Includes charts and maps.

Special Report No. **13**

THE SOON COMING BIRTH HATCHERIES

The day will come when an individual will not be allowed to have children as they wish. They will need a special permit from authorities. They will then be injected with a *"release drug"* that will allow conception to take place.

Soon guidelines will be drawn for birth hatcheries to produce genetically *"pure"* babies. Man will seek to improve on God and develop a Master Race. Human babies may be gestated in cows. Sperm banks will become a way of life.

Special Report No. **14**

QUESTIONS ASKED ME ON PROPHECY

What is meant by *"... this generation shall not pass till all these things be fulfilled"*? How does the United States fit into Bible prophecy? Who will be Antichrist?

Where will resurrected Believers live during the Millennium? Will we live again with our mates in Heaven? Are there Scriptures that show that a Believer goes to be with the Lord immediately after death? Do those who have already gone on to be with Christ know what is going on here on earth right now?

LIST quantity you desire next to each Report Number below. Reports are $1 each. Minimum order accepted is $10.

_____ 1   _____ 2   _____ 3   _____ 4   _____ 5   _____ 6   _____ 7

_____ 8   _____ 9   _____ 10   _____ 11   _____ 12   _____ 13   _____ 14

☐ ENCLOSED IS $_____ (include $1 for postage).

☐ Send me 1 copy of all 14 Reports. Enclosed is $15 ($1 for postage).

QUANTITY PRICES	
50 copies	$ 37
100 copies	$ 50
500 copies	$200
1000 copies	$300
You may mix Titles to get maximum discount.	

Mr./Mrs./Miss   Please PRINT

Address

City   State   ZIP

SALEM KIRBAN, Inc.
Kent Rd., Huntingdon Valley, Pa. 19006

LIST quantity you desire next to each Report Number below. Reports are $1 each. Minimum order accepted is $10.

RESPONSE FORM

_____ 1   _____ 2   _____ 3   _____ 4   _____ 5   _____ 6   _____ 7

_____ 8   _____ 9   _____ 10   _____ 11   _____ 12   _____ 13   _____ 14

☐ ENCLOSED IS $_____ (include $1 for postage).

☐ Send me 1 copy of all 14 Reports. Enclosed is $15 ($1 for postage).

QUANTITY PRICES	
50 copies	$ 37
100 copies	$ 50
500 copies	$200
1000 copies	$300
You may mix Titles to get maximum discount.	

Mr./Mrs./Miss   Please PRINT

Address

City   State   ZIP

SALEM KIRBAN, Inc.
Kent Rd., Huntingdon Valley, Pa. 19006